How to
EARN M
from y
PERSO
COMPUTER

How to
EARN MONEY
from your
PERSONAL
COMPUTER

Over 50 Practical Ideas

Polly Bird

PIATKUS

In memory of my mother

First published in Great Britain in 1994 by
Judy Piatkus (Publishers) Ltd of
5 Windmill Street, London W1P 1HF

**The moral rights of the author
have been asserted**

*A catalogue record for this book is available
from the British Library*

ISBN 0-7499-1416-5

Typeset from author disks by
Action Typesetting Ltd, Gloucester
Printed and bound in Great Britain by
Biddles Ltd, Guildford & King's Lynn

CONTENTS

ACKNOWLEDGEMENTS

I am grateful to the following people who agreed to be interviewed for this book: Susan Wood; Paul Evers; John Mills; Kate Hamlyn; Carrie Colliss; Jessica Beveridge; Imogen Bertin; Mary Spencer; Michael Cattell; Maureen Nield; Christine Hodgeson; Denise Howells; Louise Samuel. The Telecottage Association kindly provided information about teleworking. My thanks also go to Gill, Judy and Sarah at Piatkus, and to my agent Teresa Chris. Especial thanks are due to my husband, Jon, and my three children for their patience while this book was being written.

Polly Bird
Chester 1994

INTRODUCTION

IF YOU ARE ONE of the many thousands of people who own a home computer you may not have realised that you can use it to make money. Anyone with basic skills can use their computer to generate an income – anything from a few pounds as a hobby to a full-blown career.

Many people need or want to work from home. They may prefer the lifestyle that home working offers. They may have to look after children or an elderly person. They may have a disability that prevents them from leaving the house easily. Others may have been unemployed for some time, recently made redundant or simply want a change. Whatever the reason is for working from home, a computer is the ideal way to make money.

You may already own or have access to a computer, or you may be contemplating a new way of earning a living and are considering whether or not to buy a computer to help you do this. If you have a computer then you can read this book and get started straight away to earn money from it. If you are contemplating buying a computer, read this book to help you decide what you need to buy and what else you need to do to start making money from your computer.

Most personal computers (PCs) are grossly under-used. The children play games on them; you may do the household accounts and type a few letters. Many people have computers that are far more powerful than they need and software they have hardly used. Yet with careful application of your skills and energy, and suitable software, you can put your machine to maximum use and earn money.

This book is for everyone who wants to earn money from their PC. It will explain what kind of computer to buy, how powerful it needs to be, and what software and extra equipment you may need. It will guide you through the main types of software and the many different kinds of work you can use your computer for. It will tell you what skills you need and where to find work.

Self-employment problems and rules are also covered, and there is advice about training, and where to go for help. As you read through this book, look at the many different types of work you can do with your computer. Choose one, and start today. This is the computer age. If you have a computer you are at the forefront of technology and are well placed to use this modern marvel to your advantage.

Don't let your PC sit at home wasting space. Make it pay its way!

THE AUTHOR'S PC

As a professional writer I certainly make money from my PC, and this book was set from disk. Readers might be interested to know what equipment I use. This book was written using the Lotus AmiPro for Windows version 3.0 word processing program on an Amstrad 2386 PC that has a 65 megabyte hard disk and 4 megabytes of RAM. My printer is a Hewlett Packard DeskJet 500.

The book was then downloaded to disk in both AmiPro and ASCII; the typesetter output the camera copy for the book printer from the disk. This is not the latest technology, but it shows that you don't need to rush out and buy the latest PC to start making money.

SOFTWARE

I mention specific software to give you some idea of what is available. There are too many examples to list them all. Reading PC magazines will give you more information. When buying new software always decide what you want it to do first and then ask the vendor whether it will work on your machine.

HARDWARE AND SOFTWARE CHOICES

WHAT KIND OF COMPUTER?

THIS BOOK IS ENTITLED *How to Earn Money from your Personal Computer*, or PC. Although this can mean any computer, the term was coined by IBM and usually means IBM-compatible computers. They are computers sufficiently compatible with IBM computers that they can run the same software. These are the kind of computers that most businesses use and most people have at home for work or leisure use. You can use any home computer to start making money but a lot will depend on its capabilities and type.

The name PC is confusing because there are several other kinds of personal computers that are not referred to as PCs. Apple Macintosh computers ('Macs'), for example, are widely used by desktop publishers, designers and others who regard the Mac as having superior software and hardware for this purpose. However, the software is now very similar between the two and can even be used on both types of machines as long as suitable transfer software is installed. Many of the programs designed for the Mac have now been modified for use on PCs and vice versa.

Other computers

Other types of computer you may have at home include Archimedes, Atari and Amiga. These can all do much the same as a PC, but have the disadvantage that they are not compatible with other types of computer. This means that you cannot put a disk for a PC into an Amiga, for example, and expect it to work. However, all these computers can do most of the things mentioned in this book that involve data processing, design or word processing. But you need to be aware that they are no use to you if you want to do work with a computer that will involve using business software designed for a PC or joining a network of PCs.

If you have an Amstrad PCW this is not, strictly speaking, a PC either. A PCW is a dedicated word processor. This means that it is very good for working with text and acts rather like a glorified typewriter. Although it can now be programmed do some basic design it is not really suitable for that purpose.

Laptop PCs

Laptop PCs are portable computers. (You can also get laptop versions of other kinds of computers.) There are also even smaller notebook and palmtop computers. Laptops are at least as expensive, and sometimes more expensive than desktop computers. You can either use them on their own or some can be connected to your desktop computer so that you can transfer work done on the laptop elsewhere straight on to your home PC. Others can be used instead of a desktop PC, as well as carried about. They do have a distinct advantage over larger PCs as Imogen Bertin, a writer and designer, says:

I have a Sinclair Z88 which is one of those little notebook computers. You can type text on it and then transfer it on to your computer when you get it home. It has a silent keyboard so it's allowed in a lot of libraries.

The smaller notebook and palm-held computers are particularly useful for library work.

If you will need to collect information outside the home to use on your desktop PC you may want to consider eventually buying a laptop.

THE RIGHT SYSTEM FOR YOU

For the purposes of this book I have assumed that the computer you have gathering dust in the corner is a PC – an IBM-compatible computer. It will have a screen, a keyboard, a mouse and perhaps a joystick. It will probably have a printer. Put the joystick away. You won't need it except for playing games. Now what kind of computer do *you* need?

The system is the type of PC set-up that will suit you best for your money-making purpose. A computer consists of hardware, that is the machinery of printer, computer, mouse etc., and software which are the programs that tell the computer what to do. These are stored on small disks called floppy disks or in the computer itself on a much larger different type of disk called a hard disk. Once a floppy disk has been formatted (altered) to work on a particular type of machine it won't always work on another type. So programs for, say, an IBM computer won't work on an Atari.

There are lots of different makes but most PCs come in various types. All you need to know is that they usually have

3

numbers – 286, 386, 486 – and the larger the number the more powerful the computer. The newest models are Pentiums. They also have letters – SX and DX – the DX version runs faster.

Do not panic if your PC is not one of the most powerful. Unless speed and volume are going to be a major part of your work then one of the less powerful machines will be perfectly adequate. Bear in mind that you can never buy a state-of-the-art machine because they are changing all the time.

☐ **Don't bother to buy a new machine until your old one becomes useless for your work or falls to bits.**

If you do decide you need a new machine now then you should get one with as much RAM (random access memory) and as large a hard disk as possible. RAM is the amount of memory the computer has spare for running programs. You cannot store any information in it. The hard disk is for storing information and programs. It is measured in megabytes. A megabyte (MB) is a measure of space in the machine's memory. You do need a hard disk. Most up-to-date software requires a lot of storage space. It also needs a large amount of RAM to run. You can manage with just the small 'floppy' disks, but you will have to keep changing them as you work. A hard disk on your machine can hold many times the amount of information of a small disk. If you use Windows-based programs (described below) you will need a lot of spare memory if they are to work efficiently.

PC troubleshooter Michael Cattell, who runs a county-wide computer problem solving service, suggests a minimum size:

I use a 386 computer. That's the minimum to start
with. If you want to run modern software on it, you
can't have anything less.

4

Take Michael's advice and do not buy a new PC less than 386 size. If you can afford a bit more buy a 486DX computer with 4MB RAM and 120MB hard disk. Get more RAM and hard disk space if possible.

Always choose a machine which takes the 3.5 inch disks which are now standard. If your machine only takes 5.25 inch disks then you will need to save up for a second disk drive for the smaller size.

Screen

You will have a screen usually called a visual display unit (VDU) for your PC. If you are using the TV then you will need to buy a screen just for work. The standard for a VDU is VGA (Video Graphics Array). Anything else may be inadequate for the latest software. You will need your PC permanently set up.

In spite of what the ads tell you a monochrome screen is perfectly adequate and a lot cheaper than a colour one. Colour is only necessary if you are going to do a lot of design work or colour printing.

☐ **Get the largest screen you can afford if you are buying new.**

Printer

You may already have a printer, in which case you are all set. If not then you have three alternatives.

Dot matrix
This uses pins to press ink dots on the paper in the shape of letters. The more pins the printer uses the clearer the text will

be. Obviously a printer which uses 9 dots is going to be fuzzier than one using 24, the standard.

If you have a 24-pin dot matrix printer you can manage if you are doing something like creative writing or heavy-duty work like printing labels. But many of your clients will not welcome it. Anything less than a 24-pin is usually unacceptable nowadays.

If you are printing out work for anyone else then a dot-matrix printer will not be acceptable.

Ink jet

Ink jet machines spray dots at about 300 dpi (dots per inch). The quality is very good and the cost reasonable. You can buy colour or monochrome printers. One problem is that the printout can smudge if not handled carefully. You can buy portable printers of this type. This is the minimum standard of quality for printing out copy for somebody else.

Laser printers

Laser printers bond the ink on to the paper by heat. The copy is very clear and sharp, and this is the quality of print you must use for any high-class work such as books. The standard versions print at 300 dpi, but you can buy versions that produce copy at 600 dpi which is even sharper. Commercial concerns often use laser printers which print at 1,200 dpi. Indeed, if you have not yet bought a printer and can afford a laser printer then this would be your best buy.

Printer drivers

You may already have software installed in your computer which will allow certain types of printer to work with your machine. If not you will need to buy special software called a printer driver to enable a new printer to work. All printers have software to go with them (disks with programs on them) which tell your PC which printer is being connected and sends the instructions to it. Make sure you get the right software for the printer you choose and that it will run on your PC.

Operating systems

Computers need to have instructions in them to tell them how to work and how to use programs. The main operating system is called DOS (disk operating system). This is usually already installed in a computer. You can work well with just this system and it can be very quick to use, particularly for text. However, you have to use keyboard commands which can be time-consuming and difficult to learn and remember.

Most people now use Windows to supplement DOS. Windows is software that provides an interface between you and DOS, and makes using programs easier. It works by showing commands in the form of icons or pictures. With your mouse you can move a cursor on the screen to point to an icon. You press the button on the mouse when it is on an icon and the computer carries out whatever command the icon represents.

This is certainly much easier than using DOS on its own, although it can be a bit slower as Windows takes up a lot of memory. Most computer programs now seem to assume that you will be using Windows, although you can still get DOS-based programs. Some software comes in both DOS and Windows versions.

WHAT ELSE DO YOU NEED?

You can manage with only a screen, keyboard and printer with the appropriate software. But there are a number of other hardware choices that can add to the ease of operation and indeed may be vital depending on how you want to make money from your PC.

Mouse

The mouse is the small machine with two or three buttons connected by a cable to your PC. It is used to move a cursor around your screen in Windows-based programs. Most people now regard a mouse as standard, especially as the operating system most used is Windows. Your mouse needs the correct wire to connect it to your type of computer. For example, an Amstrad 2386 is an IBM-compatible PC, but the mouse needs to be an Amstrad mouse with a special connecting cable.

Sheet feed

If you are going to produce a great deal of printed paper then you will need a sheet feed which will feed pieces of paper into the machine one at a time for printing. If you have to feed each sheet in by hand one at a time then you are going to be wasting time. If you already have a sheet feed it may not hold enough paper for your purpose so you may need to buy an extra one. Some printers take two sheet feeds or a sheet feed and an envelope feed.

Envelope feed

The same applies to envelopes. If your work will involve printing hundreds of envelopes then an envelope feed is vital.

Label printer

You can get small printers specifically designed for printing labels. Depending on your needs, a label printer may be more useful than printing sheets of labels on your main printer.

Modem

If you are going to be connecting your phone to your computer then you will need a modem. This is a box that connects the phone and your PC. When the correct software is installed then your PC can communicate down the phone line to another PC also connected to a phone line. If you are going to be connected to a central office computer, for example, then a modem will be very important. It will also enable you to get information from central databases for a fee.

Fax

You can buy fax machines to use separately or with a telephone. But you can also buy fax 'cards' which fit inside a PC. These come with software that enables you to use your PC to fax messages via your PC as long as you have a modem. The fax machine is almost essential for any home business now, so even if you don't buy a fax card consider upgrading your phone to a combined phone/fax machine.

Scanner

A scanner is a box or hand-held tool that connects by a cable to a PC, and 'reads' pictures or diagrams and transfers them into a computer program such as a desktop publishing program. There it can be altered and moved about until it is where you want it for printing. Text can be scanned into a word processing program.

Other needs

All the bits and pieces listed below are things that fit on to your PC. But there are other things that you will need in your office to help you compete with other home-based workers.

Answering machine

An answering machine is indispensable. You cannot afford to miss offers of work because you had to go out/feed the baby/were in bed with flu. It can be combined with a fax and phone. It is also useful for freeing yourself from interruptions. You can leave it on with the sound turned up and then only lift the receiver to answer if you need to talk to the caller immediately.

Paperware

People often miss out the cost of paperware from their calculations. You are going to need a lot – paper, envelopes, labels, binders, folders etc. Use 80 gm weight of paper for most purposes or more for really quality work.

> ☐ **Buy in bulk from a discount office supply store like Office World.**

> ☐ **You *can* use fan paper (the paper with perforated sheets joined with holes down each side) and separate it after printing, but you won't create a good impression. It is better to use ordinary cut paper of decent quality. Save the fan paper for drafts or personal use.**

For labels you may need special software if your present software doesn't cater for it. Make sure it will do exactly what you need and cater for all sizes of labels.

Photocopier

Unless you are going to do a great deal of photocopying you can manage without a photocopier of your own. It is, however, convenient, if not necessarily cheaper, to have one to hand. If your photocopying needs are small then you might consider one of the cheaper small personal copiers. If you will need to do a great deal of regular photocopying then a machine may be justified. For frequent, very large runs of photocopying you will probably find it cheaper to use the services of a print shop.

SOFTWARE

Software are the programs on disks that can be installed in your computer. You will probably have some basic software such as a word processing program, spreadsheets, a database or graphics, already installed in your computer, along with some games. If this turns out to be inadequate for your needs then you will need new software. You will, however, be limited by the size of your computer's hard disk and RAM. Many software programs allow you to move data, text, pictures or diagrams from one program to another.

The standard advice about buying a computer is to buy the software first and then the computer that will use it best. But we are assuming that you already have your computer so we must tackle it from a different angle.

First of all, when you have read this book and decided what you want to do, look at your present software and see if it meets your needs. As with the hardware, the most expensive programs will not always be necessary. If your present programs are easy to use and adequate for the job then you won't need to change them.

If you do need to buy new software then first of all make a detailed list of what you want the PC to be able to do and find software to meet it. Read PC magazines such as *PC World*, *PC*

Answers or *Practical PC*, and ask a retailer's advice. But Michael Cattell says:

> Shops are guilty of selling people things that are not what they need for the sake of selling them. And when people go back the shops have got no time for them.

☐ **Retailers have a vested interest in selling you as much as possible. Make sure you only buy what *you* need to do the job.**

Always look for ease of use too. Some of the cheaper programs are not only adequate for the job, but are also much more user-friendly, while some well-known commercial programs can be fiendishly difficult to master. WordStar, for example, is a powerful word processing program which is very complicated to learn. But there are easier well-known programs such as WordPerfect or Word for Windows.

What else do you need, apart from a word processing program, to enable you to write? Consider the following.

- *Spell check/dictionary* Very useful but try to get an English (rather than American) version. It won't pick up words that are in the wrong place but spelt correctly (or keying errors that happen to make words, like 'dog' for 'God'), so you will still need to check the printed copy.
- *Thesaurus* Will provide alternatives to a word. Both this and the spell check take up a lot of space on your PC's hard disk so only install them if you need them. A book works just as well!
- *Spreadsheet* Needed for accounting work. Can be complicated for novices to learn.
- *Database* Can be very useful for saving and accessing lots of information, e.g. lists of customers, but again difficult to learn.

- *Graphic packages* Useful only if you need to provide good quality diagrams or pictures.
- *Desktop publishing (DTP) programs* Be careful of these. If your word processing program will do most things you need, then you may not need to buy one. Ami Pro, for example, is almost a DTP program in itself. If you are going to be doing a lot of fine page design, however, then you will need one. There are many cheap packages that will produce nice leaflets and newsletters.
- *Mail merge* Very important if you are going to do a lot of personalised mail or envelopes. It will insert information in a basic format chosen by you. You know all those direct mail letters starting 'Dear Mrs Smith of 13 Forgotten Way . . .'!
- *Labels software* Again very useful if you are going to produce a lot of labels. It can be used with mail merge programs.

Connected software

You will need specific software to use a modem and a fax with a PC. These should be provided with the products. Make sure the disk size is correct for your machine.

Shareware and public domain programs

There are many public-spirited enthusiasts out there who enjoy making programs and who are willing to make them available to the public for a small fee or even for free. Shareware programs are those which you can 'try before you buy' for a few pounds. If you then decide you like them you can pay another fee to register as a user, and get the full manuals and upgraded versions. Public domain programs are available to anyone for free.

Shareware relies heavily on trust and should not be abused. You will find it advertised in PC magazines.

☐ Shareware programs are usually aimed at solving very specific programming needs and are often much easier to use than commercial programs.

2

BEFORE YOU START – COMPUTER VIRUSES

THE PROBLEM OF COMPUTER VIRUSES is very important not only to you but also to your customers or employer. Failure to take account of this phenomenon could result in the loss of not only your own work but also that of anyone who gives you a disk with their hard-won information on it to use in your machine. Although the loss of data because of a computer virus is comparatively rare at the moment, it is becoming more common and the consequences can be dire.

WHAT IS THE PROBLEM?

It is an unfortunate fact that there are some people who enjoy the challenge of creating computer programs that will destroy your work or render your computer operating system useless, or merely cause intense irritation and interrupt your work. These invasive programs are called computer viruses and, like their biological counterparts, they can move from host to host, that is, from disk to disk.

A virus is a program that the program creator has secretly embedded in software. Your PC is most likely to get it, if at all, by means of a corrupted floppy disk. When loaded, the virus tries to copy itself on to your computer system and interfere with it. If it succeeds it will make your programs behave oddly at unexpected times. Once embedded in your hard disk the virus can then infect other floppy disks. Some viruses simply copy themselves repeatedly until they have filled up your disk space and so slow down the system. Others take control of your machine and cause malicious damage. For example, one makes all the letters on your screen fall to the bottom. Another, the 'Michelangelo virus', is programmed to destroy all the information in your PC on the date of the artist's birthday. The problem is that if you get a virus on your disk and therefore into the computer memory it can infect any other work you do on the PC. PC users have had all their information destroyed in this way. What may be a joke for the virus creator is a nightmare for users.

Some viruses are not immediately obvious when you first use a disk but they become embedded in the PC's memory and can emerge some time later, sometimes at a specific date. While they are in your machine they can infect any other disk which you use.

Not only can you transfer a virus to your PC by using an infected disk, it can also enter by other means. Using a modem can allow a virus to contaminate your PC. Because it involves connecting your PC to another via a phone line you risk allowing a virus to enter your PC in this way. If your PC is connected to a network of other PCs then if one PC becomes contaminated then the whole network is vulnerable.

Fortunately most computer viruses are harmless or irritating. Nevertheless you can waste a great deal of time and energy in trying to deal with them.

The danger if you work at home with your PC is obvious.

It would be bad enough if it was only your own disks that were affected. But if you are accepting disks from other people to use in your machine or are sending work back to clients on disk then you risk presenting them with unusable data and corrupting their computers. This will not endear you to clients and you will lose business. It could also possibly leave you open to a risk of being sued.

Any disk you use needs to be free from viruses, as does any disk you send back to your clients.

HOW CAN YOU FIGHT THEM?

Fortunately for us, virus creators are not the only people out there who are experts on computer viruses. There are programmers who spend their time creating software to counter viruses. Their job is to identify each virus program, called a strain, and to create another program that will destroy it. This is an ongoing job because as the anti-virus programmers identify each virus strain, the virus creators change it or develop a new one, so the virus killers have to amend their own programs.

Your first action on deciding to use a PC to work with from home should be to buy a combined virus-scanner and virus-killer program, and to make sure that it is up to date and updated regularly.

☐ **Buy the most recent version you can find and choose one that offers regular upgrades.**

Examples of anti-virus software include Microsoft Anti-

Virus, Norton Anti-Virus for DOS, Dr Solomon's Anti-Virus Toolkit and F-Prot Anti-Virus.

WHAT SHOULD YOU DO TO AVOID VIRUSES?

There are three things that you need to do regularly to ensure the safety of your work and that of your clients when disks are used. The first is to be careful about the disks you use. Then you should scan all disks for signs of a virus. Finally, if you find a virus, you must activate a virus-killing program to destroy the virus.

Even if you have bought a program to deal with your viruses there is a basic precaution you should take at all times. To put it simply, do not use any disk in your computer unless it has come from a reliable source such as a major commercial software manufacturer who will have automatically checked all disks for all known viruses before putting them on sale.

If you obtain disks from shareware or public domain advertisements, download programs from computer bulletin boards or are given them by friends then you will need to check them. You should also check disks given away free on the front of magazines. If in doubt about the source or reliability of any program or disk, do not use it without checking it for viruses.

Be wary about letting other people use your machine, unless you are confident of their reliability and know that they only use disks approved by you. You need to know what disks go in and out of your machine.

☐ Do not to let your children play games on your PC if you are working with it from home. This may seem cruel but children often obtain disks from unreliable sources or get copies of disks that their friends use in their computers. You therefore run the risk of letting a virus into your PC if they use your machine. The same applies to disks that colleagues offer to copy for you at work or offer to lend you.

If your PC at home is the family's game machine then consider either buying another for your own use or buying them another one with your first earnings. It will not only mean that you have sole access to your PC for work without having to elbow aside the rest of the family, but you can also be reasonably sure that your PC can remain free of viruses.

Virus scanning

Virus-killing programs are normally combined with virus-scanning programs. This kind of program checks the hard disk of your computer, ideally every time you switch it on, scans the floppy disks you use in the computer for viruses when they are inserted and takes note of any unusual signs from within the computer that might suggest a virus is present.

If you are going to put other people's disks into your machine, whether for word processing purposes, file conversion or any other reason, make sure that you check each one for a virus. You need to buy anti-virus software and use it for each disk you receive, and get it to check your PC's hard disk each time you switch it on. This way you will find out immediately if you need to take further action. In the same way you should check every disk you send out so that you can say that your disks have been checked for viruses.

Virus killing

If your virus-scanner program detects a virus in your PC then you must activate the virus-killing program if this does not occur automatically. This must be done immediately and *before* you put any further work into the PC.

Any good anti-virus program will claim that it can check for all *known* viruses. This will be true at the time of producing the program. But since computer viruses are constantly changing, you must buy regular upgrade programs because the anti-virus programmers will have amended and created new programs to cope with the new strains. If you do not upgrade this kind of software regularly then you risk a new virus entering your PC system that your present software cannot cope with.

IS ANTI-VIRUS SOFTWARE EXPENSIVE?

A brand-name anti-virus program could cost as little as £10 or as much as £295, but will be priceless in terms of peace of mind. And how much will your work be worth to you? Days of data worth hundreds of pounds in business could be rendered useless – money that you won't see if a virus has got at your work. If you are going to use your PC for making money then good anti-virus software should be a priority purchase.

3

WORD PROCESSING THAT PAYS

THE COMPUTER REVOLUTION means that many people have keyboard skills which they can use to make money with their PC at home. You can now type on to a computer using a word processing package, and the text can be altered and re-arranged on screen. This is called word processing and encompasses not only the traditional typing skills, but also the ability to use computer programs and commands to lay out the text. As many word processing programs also include the ability to produce simple tables and diagrams, this too has become part of the word processing domain.

WHAT IS WORD PROCESSING?

Word processing encompasses not just the typing of text on to a computer keyboard so that it appears on the screen, but also arranging it in such a way that it looks good. It has the advantage over typing that everything is altered and corrected on the screen so that only a perfect version is printed. As many copies of that version as required can be printed with little effort on the part of the keyboard operator. You can store the text in the PC's memory for as long as necessary and reprint it again at a later date.

Typical word processing utilities include the ability to produce centred, justified and right-aligned text, set tabs, and create bold, italic and underlined text in a variety of fonts (type styles), as well as in different sizes. The more modern programs allow you to drag text around the screen and drop it into place.

Many programs also allow you to do much more, such as creating columns and tables, and simple drawings. Some of the most powerful word processing packages are almost a complete desktop publishing (DTP) system in their own right.

Style sheets and templates

A good word processing program will also include style sheets or templates. These two terms are often used interchangeably. They define the text styles of a document and dictate where the text, and sometimes illustrations, should go. For example, you might have a style sheet for a business letter, a memo, an invoice or a fax sheet. This makes it easy for anyone to produce a good-looking document with minimum effort or room for mistakes.

If you want to produce a document using a style sheet or template all you need to do is to call the appropriate style sheet from the program on to your screen and key in your text. Your words automatically appear in a predetermined size and style, and are placed in pre-set positions. The result is a perfect, well-designed document ready for printing. You can also create your own style sheets or modify existing ones.

☐ Use style sheets or templates whenever possible.

Be proud of your skills!

There is nothing degrading about offering straightforward word processing skills equivalent to typing skills – it is a vital job. For those people who want to offer more than simple typing of documents to produce well laid-out, accurate copy, the classic secretarial skills of dictation (from a tape) and composing letters can be added. But be careful how you describe your work. Susan Wood runs a word processing and typing service. She says:

> I include the word typing so as not to confuse my older customers. I don't call myself a secretarial service because then people would expect me to take dictation over the phone, send their faxes, book flights for them and so on. I don't have the equipment to offer that. I offer plain typing and CVs. I do things from straightforward little letters to books to complicated tables and invoices.

WHAT SKILLS DO YOU NEED?

The skills you can offer will depend on what skills you already have and what you are prepared to obtain. Obviously, typing at a reasonable speed and with accuracy is important. So is an understanding of the commands of whatever word processing program you are using. You could also offer to transcribe shorthand notes and type them up, do audio typing, type labels and envelopes, etc.

The basic skills you need are typing/keyboard skills, shorthand, accuracy and speed. You may need audio typing skills as well, that is, being able to type from taped information. You need to be neat, be able to correct inaccurate grammar and present the result in clean, collated printout. Take Susan Wood's advice:

> If anyone wants to do my kind of work I would definitely recommend that they do some typing training, knowing how to handle people's work. You get such a lot of variation that you've got to know how to handle each piece of work separately. It isn't a case of putting it up on a screen and just bashing it out: you've got to be thinking about everything. You have to think do they want them bound, is it a business letter, should it not have 'Dear Sir, Yours faithfully'? You've got to know how to change people's work, their natural errors, so you've got to be very good at English as well.
>
> It isn't a case of you've got the machine so go and do it, you've got to have had some background to make a success of it otherwise you'll slip up and you'll lose your clients straight away.

EQUIPMENT

You already have your computer, keyboard and printer. You will need a mouse if your word processing program is Windows based. You may want to add additional software that includes a spell check and grammar check. Grammar check programs have their limitations but can be useful for picking up lower case letters at the beginning of sentences or badly constructed simple sentences. Susan Wood's equipment is typical:

> I use an IBM type 486 computer and I work with both a DOS and a Windows program. My printer is a DeskJet. The printer is mono. I don't have much call for colour. I don't have a fax. Writers send me their work by post and I have a lot of local clients.

If you are going to type envelopes or labels you may need to buy software to cope with that, and envelope and label feeds for your printer. If you can offer audio typing skills then you will need a tape player, preferably one that works with a foot pedal, as well as headphones. A paper rest, foot rest and arm rest will make sure that you do not overstrain yourself. A good typist's chair is important, as well as a VDU screen for your computer.

Your paper and envelopes should be good quality 80 gm weight. Anything less looks cheap and you will need to offer good-quality work to professional and office clients.

TYPES OF WORK

Word processing work on a computer can involve many different things. Basically the ability to key in/type given words in set forms is important, although if you are a skilled secretary you may be asked to compose letters and memos yourself from notes. There are particular ways of setting out different types of document, so a basic typing course would be very useful.

Letters

Letters will be printed out on the headed paper of the company from which you obtain the work. Your clients should supply you with enough for the job. If you are asked to supply your own paper, use good-quality bond of at least 80 gm, if not more, for top copies. Find out from your customers how many top copies and second copies they need. Second or 'bottom' copies can be printed on thinner paper if required.

Make sure you are clear about how your clients want letter headings and letters set out. This may seem a simple point but some firms still like indented paragraphs, for example, whereas many prefer all left-hand margins aligned. If possible, ask for examples of existing letters, memos etc., so that you can follow the preferred style.

Always check for spelling and grammar even if the writer hasn't, and always provide the top copy and at least one extra copy, more if the client asks for it.

Theses/dissertations

Students are a good source of theses and dissertations, and here the required skills are slightly different. Obviously, accuracy and neatness are important, but you must also be able to decipher bad typing or handwriting. You will need to supply at least two, sometimes three, copies of the document within a specific time limit. This is important because the student has to get the work in by a certain date in order for it to count towards their final award. If you take on this kind of work you must be sure that you can keep to the deadlines stated.

Phone up and check if there is anything you don't understand. Don't guess what it means. And follow the format required – this is specifically laid down by the university or college and should not be altered.

Articles

Articles are much shorter than dissertations but often have to be completed very quickly, possibly overnight. Not many writers nowadays ask someone else to type their work but a few still do, especially if they have several projects to complete quickly. Articles must be typed double-spaced with margins of at least 3 cm.

Books

The page numbering of a book manuscript must be through from the first page after the title page to the end, not numbered within each chapter. Double spacing is vital again. Each chapter must start on a new page. Do not overlook the title page, contents, dedication at the front and bibliography, notes and appendices at the back.

The trouble with books is that they are long! And two copies at least are required. You may get involved with the book and enjoy reading it as you go along. On the other hand it could be awful. Fortunately, it is not your job to comment on the literary merit or otherwise of any work you are sent. If the author asks you what you think of the book, it is better to maintain a neutral stance.

> ☐ **Check words or phrases you are not sure of. What seems incorrect may be a carefully intended insertion into the book.**

Plays and screen scripts

Plays and screen scripts have to be set out somewhat differently from articles or books in order to make clear the distinction between stage directions and speech. *Writing a Play* by Steve Gooch (A & C Black, 1988) will give you suitable guidelines. If the playwright you are working for has written other plays, ask to see an example so that you can copy the layout.

Reports

You may be asked to put company reports in a nice cover, in which case you will need to have plenty of card or plastic folders that you can label. Or you can buy folders with pockets for business cards and ask the company to supply you with cards to put in them.

Use good-quality paper, and make sure that you number pages and footnotes correctly.

Providing work on disk

Now that publishers have moved into the computer age many authors are asked to submit their work on disk. You can easily supply a copy of the printed work (the hard copy), as well as a copy on a disk, for a specified fee. Ask what computer language you should use for your client's disk. If you do not have a word processing package that will translate your word processing text into the required language, change it into ASCII (American Standard Code for Information Interchange), a simple language which can be read by virtually all computers.

CVs

There is a market for well-produced CVs (curriculum vitae). In these days of mass unemployment a well-designed CV can make the difference between work and the dole. Because this is a popular PC money-making business and can be produced both by using word processing software, as well as specially designed programs, I am considering it separately here.

What is a CV?

Curriculum vitae (CV for short) means 'course of one's life', and is a written sketch of a person's life and achievements until the date of writing it. It commonly includes details of work, education, interests and achievements. It is sent to prospective employers to try and persuade them to give the subject of the CV a job.

Now that good-quality printed matter is such a ubiquitous part of everyday life employers have high expectations of how CVs are presented. While they may ask for a covering letter in the applicant's own handwriting, the CV itself has to be clear and attractive.

What goes in a CV?

A good CV is clear, well written, imaginative where possible (but truthful!) and geared to the particular job being sought. It should tell the applicant's work history in chronological order and be kept to one or two pages at the most. It should be typed on good-quality paper. There is a set formula for the first page of a CV. The client's full name should be at the top, together with details of the job applied for. Then these details should follow in this order.

- Full name, address and telephone number.
- Personal details (date of birth, age, marital status, country of birth, full address).
- Names, addresses and phone numbers of your referees.
- Jobs done in date order starting with the most recent and working backwards, together with a description of the

work involved, and the name and address of employer. Any gaps should have a brief reason given.

- Education and qualifications gained (secondary school, college, university, other courses), again in reverse date order.
- Any other expertise relevant to the job.
- Hobbies/interests.

What can you offer?

You can offer simply to type out a CV to the customer's demand and merely give advice on presentation. A CV can be produced in an attractive manner with a word processing program and many clients will be satisfied with this. Others will want you to suggest how to word a CV and what to put in it.

Can you cater for content?

You may want to confine yourself simply to producing what the client wants. If you have skills in writing you may be able to suggest ways of phrasing the information so that the client is presented in the best possible light. Unless you are confident of your skill in wording the document, stick to offering a nicely produced CV to the client's specifications. Even this will be valuable to people who would otherwise struggle to produce their CV with a typewriter or fountain pen. Susan Wood says:

> CVs are quite a speciality of mine. I offer lots of variations on layouts and other things. I do give advice on those. I advise on the laying out, not on their content because I'm not a careers adviser.

If you feel that you would like to offer your customers something more than just simple typing of a CV then you must take time and trouble. You must discuss with your client what should go in it. Have they missed out any basic facts? If so, you must point this out to them because, however beautifully you type their CV, they will have less chance of the job if vital information is missing.

There is more to a CV than just filling in details of education, employment and so on. You do need to have an understanding of how best to convey your client's expertise and good points while playing down (but not being dishonest about) the negative points. Tom Jackson's *The Perfect CV* (Piatkus, 1991) is a useful introduction to the subject.

Ready-programmed CV software

There are now a number of software packages that are ready-programmed to produce attractive CVs in a variety of different formats. All you need to be able to do is key in your client's information into the relevant part of the CV, check it for spelling and print it out. You can give your customer a choice of designs and be satisfied with that.

You could also offer to check for grammatical mistakes, reword obviously clumsy language and, again, offer advice as to content.

The advantage of these ready-made programs is that the designing has all been taken care of, leaving you to concentrate on the content.

For more on ready-made programs, see Chapter 11.

Problems

Producing nice-looking CVs is a good way of using your PC to make money but there are problems. First of all, do not offer to advise on content unless you have had a lot of experience in this field or you have had training in career advice. If you make a mess of the content your clients will blame you for their continuing failure to find a job. If, however, you do feel capable of doing this then you can charge a lot more for your service than for simply typing the CV.

A spell checker and/or a good knowledge of English is very important. You should not allow your clients to be left open to embarrassment because they have spelt something wrong and you have blindly copied it. Even if it is their fault, make the corrections.

WHERE TO FIND WORK

You should be able to find word processing work from local firms. These may be small firms that cannot afford full-time secretarial staff, or large firms needing cover for absentees or extra work in a busy period. For theses and dissertations put cards up at all the local colleges. If you fancy typing books or articles then take out a small ad in the writing magazines and professional journals such as *The Author*, *Writers News*, *Writers Forum*.

You can also advertise in the classified section of the local papers. Don't forget the freesheets and look especially for the business sections. These may only appear every few weeks and are aimed directly at the local business community.

Send out a simple leaflet to local clubs and organisations who might be grateful for secretarial help.

Why not join your local business club if there is one? This will bring you in contact with potential clients and give you an insight into their secretarial needs.

TIMING

Don't assume that you will have a steady flow of work all the time. Even secretarial work is seasonal. Theses and dissertations will bring you work in the spring, while you will be asked to provide holiday cover in the summer. Try to have a mixture of work so that you have something bringing in money all the year round.

EARNINGS

You can charge per hour or per 1000 words. Each copy will be a bit cheaper. You could charge by the word for theses, dissertations, articles and books, and by the hour for letters, memos and reports. Add postage if customers are not collecting their work, and the cost of labels, envelopes, folders etc.

If you are offering other services such as printing and storing names and addresses then you could charge a flat hourly rate.

4

WRITING FOR PROFIT

You can not only make money from your PC by typing other people's work. With ideas and application you can produce saleable writing of your own using your PC.

Writing needs hard work and enthusiasm as well as talent. But with your PC the physical act of getting words on to paper becomes easier. Your output increases and therefore so does your income. Writer Maureen Nield has found that using a PC is profitable *and* fun:

> For me, buying a word processor proved a shrewd financial and creative investment. Once over the temptation to fiddle with fonts and play Picasso with Paintbrush, I found the sheer logic of its working concentrated my mind wonderfully. True, the first, free-ranging draft is still done with pen and paper, but seeing the result on screen and finally back on paper (but in print!) is still a wonderfully morale-boosting experience. It makes one feel that the next stage has simply *got* to be between the covers on a bookshop shelf.

EQUIPMENT

The equipment necessary for profitable writing has always been very simple. Years ago a pen and paper were the only tools needed, then a typewriter and now a computer. But you do not need a powerful computer or a complicated word processing program to produce good copy. Journalist and business writer, Kate Hamlyn, has found this to be true:

> I use an Epson EL2 computer. It only has a 64 megabyte hard disk and it's not very fast. The software I use is Word 5.0 which is fairly old-fashioned but does the job. My printer is a Canon Bubble Jet.

And, as I have said in the introduction, this book was not written on the most up-to-date PC either.

If you have not already chosen word processing software, have a look at what is available for your computer before you buy and install any. For creative writing you need to be able to do the following:

- set a page template or style sheet;
- alter margins;
- number pages;
- set spacing;
- move text.

If you like you can also look for a program which offers:

- word counting;
- spell checking;
- thesaurus;
- dictionary.

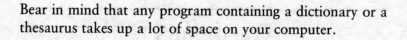
Bear in mind that any program containing a dictionary or a thesaurus takes up a lot of space on your computer.

☐ **Even today you may find a book better value than a dictionary program!**

Once you have chosen your program, spend some time working through the manual and getting to know it. It is irritating to get half-way through a piece of writing and discover that you cannot remember how to use the spell check or produce underlining.

☐ **Although most programs can cope with a lot of fancy effects like italics and bold letters, you do not need them. Underline words if you want the editor to treat them as italics and do not use bold at all.**

Printer choices

The most important piece of equipment for a creative writer after the word processing software and computer is the printer. More and more editors prefer not to look at dot matrix printout, even though these printers have improved beyond measure. They do not like the 'dottiness' of the print. If you have a 9-pin dot matrix printer try to save up as soon as possible for a 24-pin version that gives an acceptable quality.

Ink jet printers are good, medium-priced printers. They are sturdy and reliable, and the print quality is very good. If you can afford to splash out then buy a laser printer but remember that you will only need it for producing text so you do not need to buy the most expensive. Make sure you keep it well maintained and set aside some money for printing ink-cartridges. Kate Hamlyn says:

One problem that can occur is the printer going wrong. If a typewriter goes wrong you can just pull the paper out and start again. If the printer packs up it's difficult to get access to what you've written. You don't notice the cost of using a computer but when you go to buy a new printer cartridge it can be a shock.

Paper

You should use 80 gm paper for top copies. But you can save on paper in other ways. Kate Hamlyn has this tip:

You can save on typing paper because you don't waste paper typing endless drafts to be corrected. I recycle paper to use for drafts.

Spare disks

You will need plenty of spare disks. It is surprising how much work disks can hold, but you will find you use them up quickly, especially if you write novels or want to keep different types of writing on different disks. Always keep back-up copies of your disk either on another disk or on your machine's hard disk if it has one. Your computer manual will tell you how to do this. If you accidentally wipe out the information in your computer or the computer breaks down you will lose all your work unless you have a back-up copy. This, together with your hard copy, will ensure that if you do leave your disk on a bus or lose the printout in the post you always have another copy to use.

Skills Needed

There are certain things that you need for writing apart from creative talent. The formula of 1 per cent inspiration and 99 per cent perspiration is an accurate assessment of a writer's work.

Check your work

You need to be able to write clear, grammatical English and spell correctly. Some word processing programs will provide you with a spell checker and/or a thesaurus, but they are no substitute for checking your work yourself.

People who do have a spell checker as part of their word processing programs tend to assume that they can leave the job to the computer. While the program will pick up incorrectly spelt words it will not pick out words that are correctly spelt but in the wrong place or incorrect punctuation. (Eye two am aloud two bee one of yew!) You can produce perfectly spelt copy on your computer that nevertheless does not make sense.

☐ **Check your work on hard copy (the printout). It is easy to miss mistakes on a screen however careful you are. Printing out your work occasionally to check for mistakes is a wise precaution.**

If possible, get someone else to check it too. Always keep a hard copy of your work in any case – you never know when you will lose all your disks or your computer will get broken.

Neatness counts

As well as basic literacy skills you will need to be neat. Editors of any kind of creative writing will only look at neatly typed or printed writing. This is where your computer scores over the typewriter. You can set out a basic style sheet according to the kind of writing you are doing, and use it again and again. You can choose your typeface, spacing and style of page numbering. You can shift words about and cut them out without having to retype them each time. In the end you can produce as many copies as you like of perfectly spelt and printed work.

PRESENTATION

Writing for publication and profit also involves setting out your work in a particular way. Your work should be double-spaced with margins of at least 3 cm all round. Type your name, address and phone number, and the number of words in the top right-hand corner of the first page. Type the title and your name a third of the way down the page. Leave a couple of lines and then start your writing. Indent all paragraphs, except the first, at the beginning. Type the word 'end' centred under the last sentence, and repeat your name and address in the bottom left-hand corner. Number the pages starting with the first page. With each number put a catch line such as a word from the title and your name, e.g. Earn/Bird-3. Staple or paperclip the pages together.

If you are writing a novel or a story you will need a cover sheet. This should have your details in the top right-hand corner. A third of the way down type the title followed with 'by (your name)' and in the bottom left-hand corner put an approximate word count.

For a novel remember that each chapter must start on a new page, but number the pages from one to the end through the chapters. Do not start each chapter with page number 1.

The format for poetry is different. Use single-spacing, and double-spacing between verses or stanzas. Centre the poem in the middle of the sheet. You do not need to state the number of words or use a cover sheet.

Plays should be set out in a standard style which clearly distinguishes dialogue from narrative.

Counting words

Words mean money for writers because each project is written to a specific length. You may have a word-count facility in your program, but don't worry if you haven't. Editors are used to working with approximate word counts. Simply count the number of words in ten full lines in your typescript and divide by ten to get the average number of words. Count the number of lines on three full pages (if your program cannot do it for you) and divide by three to get the average number of lines per page. Then multiply the average number of words by the average number of lines per page by the number of pages (count incomplete pages as whole ones).

HOW TO SEND YOUR WORK

You can pack your novel or other work in a computer paper or typing paper box together with a covering letter and a self-addressed stamped label for return. Fold articles once and put them in a B5 envelope with a self-addressed stamped envelope (SASE). You can fold poems three times and put in a DL envelope with a SASE.

Covering letter

It is polite and helpful to the editor to send a covering letter. But keep it short. Simply say something along the lines of 'I enclose a poem/novel/article called xxxxx of approximately xxx words for your consideration. I enclose a SASE in case of rejection.' (See page 45 for non-fiction books.) Always send return postage however rich you think the publisher or magazine is. It is an accepted courtesy and failure to do so will mean you not only lose your manuscript but will also reduce your chances of publication. The fact that you can run off innumerable copies of the work on your computer is irrelevant. It is only polite to encourage the editors to reply to your unsolicited efforts at your expense.

WRITING SKILLS

If you want to improve your writing skills there are a number of courses you can take. Your local adult education classes will probably provide tuition in a wide range of writing skills which could be anything from basic letter writing and grammar, to comprehensive courses on poetry or fiction writing. You can find details about these at your local library or in your regional course listings magazine, such as London's *Floodlight*.

Residential or 'holiday' writing courses are popular and are often advertised in writers' magazines. Typically these provide some class work and some personal tutorials over a period of a weekend or a week with plenty of free time. They vary in quality but some such as the *Arvon Foundation* or *Ty Newydd* courses in creative writing have a good reputation (see '*Useful addresses*' at the back of this book). Your regional arts board should be able to tell you of other similar courses in your area.

There are many correspondence courses in creative writing advertised in writing magazines and the national press. These can differ a great deal in quality depending on the expertise of the tutors and the value you get for your money. It is wise to make careful checks about the effectiveness of any course you are interested in, what you will be getting for your money and how long you can take to do the course. The London School of Journalism provides correspondence writing courses at the end of which students receive a diploma.

Finally there are the part-time or full-time college courses such as the University of East Anglia's degree in creative writing. You can find details about these courses and the qualifications you need by checking in your library for books on university and college admissions.

When you do tackle your own writing there are certain things you will need to bear in mind about the different forms.

Poetry

Everyone thinks they can write poetry. Many people can and many more write poems but are too afraid to send them out for publication.

When you have written some poems that please you, send between two and six to a magazine of your choice with the usual covering letter and SASE. Expect to wait a long time for a reply because poetry magazines are often run by one person and the guinea pig.

If your poetry is accepted you will wait even longer for publication and the rewards are few. Usually a copy of the magazine is the payment, although some offer a few pounds in remuneration.

Commercial magazines sometimes publish poetry – have a look at a few or check in the *Writers' and Artists' Yearbook* (A & C Black, annual). They pay more, but it is notoriously difficult to get published by them.

If you fancy your chances in book form you may be doomed

to failure. The few commercial publishers such as Oxford University Press or Faber take very few poets on and then only if they have had years of success in magazines and journals, and perhaps publication by one of the smaller poetry publishers. But you can try. Send out about 40 pages of poetry with a covering letter and return postage – but don't hold your breath. You can also try the main poetry-only publishers, such as Bloodaxe or Carcanet. There are many smaller firms who may publish you and ask for help with production fees. Find out how much you may be asked to pay before you go ahead.

Stories

There is still a demand for short stories, although more and more women's magazines in particular are using American authors. Study the type of story your preferred publication uses. Check the required length in the magazine and in the *Writers' and Artists' Yearbook* or *The Writer's Handbook*, and send your stories to the fiction editor. Payment varies depending on the magazine, at a rate per 1,000 words.

Articles

Keep strictly to the word length stated in the magazines' guidelines in the writers' handbooks. You can send out a query letter first. This is a one-page letter, single-spaced, giving details of your article ideas and asking whether the editor would like to see your completed article.

Using the phone

You may need to use the telephone a lot if you need to include interviews in your articles. Kate Hamlyn says:

> As a journalist I can work at home using my
> computer. But you do need a lot of good contacts.

You have to know editors; it's not enough to be good and to know other journalists. Some kinds of journalists, such as financial journalists, need to get out and meet people at results meetings, press conferences and so on. It's important to hear gossip so working at home isn't ideal. Journalists who work at home use the telephone a great deal.

Plays

You can write plays for the stage, TV or radio. Plays must also fit into a set time limit, so it is important to time the speaking and action that takes place.

The BBC produces a useful leaflet 'Writing Plays for Radio' obtainable from the Literary Manager (Radio Drama) BBC, Broadcasting House, Portland Place, London W1A 1AA. A & C Black publish useful books on writing for radio and television.

Try writing stage plays for your local drama group and then offer work to repertory companies. Contact them first to find out what kind of plays they are looking for and how many actors they like to use.

Novels

No computer will write your story for you in spite of what many people hope! But your PC can help you organise your thoughts. Some word processing programs have an outline mode which can help you to organise the framework of your book.

Never send the whole manuscript in unsolicited. Send a synopsis of the novel (that is a few pages with details of the character and the plot) and no more than two sample chapters. Using a computer makes it easy to print out the whole thing for a new publisher if the first rejects your work.

Non-fiction books

Non-fiction is easier to sell but it must be on a subject you know about (or can find out a lot about) and you must have an angle that is different from other books presently in the shops.

Write a synopsis and give a chapter-by-chapter breakdown of the content. In a letter tell the publisher whom the book is aimed at, why it is different and why you are best qualified to write it. Don't write the complete book unless a publisher gives you a contract. Publishers often have particular formats for non-fiction or ideas of their own about what should go in a book. If you let them tell you their ideas before you write, then you will not waste time producing unsuitable work.

The rewards vary from publisher to publisher, and on the type of book and the fame of the author. A good non-fiction book can often stay in print much longer than fiction because of its ongoing usefulness and interest. School text books in particular often stay in print for years.

☐ **Before sending your book synopsis to a publisher, phone first to gauge their interest.**

Vanity presses

Whatever you are writing do not send it to a vanity press unless you wish to pay out large sums of money. These presses advertise that they are looking to publish writing but then accept anyone who will pay their large printing fees. Some writers who have used them have found themselves broke, with half their books unbound and no publicity organised. No legitimate publisher is so desperate that they need to advertise – why should they when they are inundated daily with unsolicited work?

If you cannot interest a publisher, then why not publish the book yourself? Take your printout to several local printers for an estimate. Organise publicity yourself and you may have a better chance of selling it.

WHERE TO FIND WORK

Two good books of markets are the *Writers' and Artists' Yearbook* published annually by A & C Black and the *Writers' Handbook* edited by Barry Turner (Macmillan). An excellent list of markets for freelance journalists is in *1000 Markets for Freelance Writers* by Robert Palmer (Piatkus, 1993). There is also a writers' magazine *Freelance Writers News* that gives details of new markets. Magazines like *Writers News* and *Writers Monthly* give hints on writing and information about new prospects.

EARNINGS

A poem may earn you a copy of the magazine it appears in or a small fee. Try poetry competitions. Read the rules carefully and obey them. Pay the fee and put your name and address on a separate piece of paper attached to your poem so that it can be judged without your identity being known. The prizes in poetry competitions can range from a few pounds to several hundreds with the Arvon/Observer National Poetry competition heading the league. Basically, though, if you write poetry, be prepared to be poor.

The NUJ sets standard rates for its members for articles and these act as guidelines for the publishers. The writers' handbooks give details. However, if editors can get away with paying you less they will. Writers can often get more than the standard rates, especially if they have experience. Payments vary widely.

Books, both fiction and non-fiction, are paid by an advance on royalties and then royalties. Royalties are a percentage of the price of the book. You will get some of this money before the book is sold, usually half on signing the contract and half on delivery of the typescript. When the sales of the book have paid off your advance then you will receive a royalty on each book sold. There are other rights to consider − foreign rights, book club rights etc. If you don't have an agent then you can ask the Society of Authors to look at your contract. This is one of the advantages of joining the Society. The same applies to non-fiction books. When you are successful you can try asking an agent to take you on. A list of agents appears in both writers' handbooks.

5

MONEY FROM DATA PROCESSING

ONE PIECE OF SOFTWARE that is commonly used on computers nowadays is a data processing package. Although aimed at business users it can be a very useful program for anyone who wants to use their PC to make money. It can be used as a tool to help in other work or as a profit spinner in its own right. Lists compiled on a database can be sold on (see Chapter 6) or used to compile catalogues, personnel and membership lists, and even books.

WHAT IS A DATABASE?

A database is a collection of connected pieces of information such as an address list, information about customers or a book list. Before the advent of the computer, information of this kind was commonly stored in a card file in alphabetical or other sequence. When a piece of information needed to be retrieved it involved sorting through the cards individually until the required card was reached.

A database on a computer is the same thing except that

electronic storage and retrieval makes the process much easier and quicker. It is particularly good for storing records that contain a lot of text or a combination of text and numbers. Many databases can contain any number of records up to the limit of your PC's hard disk storage space.

Information is stored as separate records for each single entity, such as a person, just as you would use a file card or record card. Each piece of information on a database 'record card' is given its own name. This is called a field name. So, for example, on each 'card' in a membership list database you might have information with the field names 'Address' and 'Name'. This is then stored in a computer file. When information needs to be retrieved the user can command the computer to search for a particular piece of information by specifying certain criteria, for example, all customers living in Yorkshire. The information can then be read off the screen or printed out.

One advantage of storing information on a computer database is that you can design the layout of the cards yourself and make them any size you like.

☐ **Design your file card on paper before creating one on screen.**

The major disadvantage of using a database is that you have to type in a lot of information before it becomes useful. But once set up it can pay you dividends in the time and effort needed to extract the information.

Storing databases on a computer has the advantage of making sorting into any order easy. For example, you could sort alphabetically, numerically, by location or name.

Flat-file and relational databases

A database that is designed to be used on its own is called a flat-file database. This is suitable for such things as basic contact lists, and straightforward querying and reporting of information. As these types of files become large they get more unwieldy and difficult to maintain.

For more sophisticated tasks you need one of the more advanced databases that enable different databases with connecting material to be joined. These are called relational databases. They enable you to keep information in smaller more manageable files and then connect the information when needed. For instance, if you had a list of customers and a list of the products they buy, you could produce invoices using data from both tables linked through a 'relation' or a shared field that the databases have in common. This common field is called a 'join-field'. So in one join-field you might use numbers to represent a customer. So a customer might be 123 in the common join-field called 'ID' and on another database would perhaps be products that the customer buys, each with his ID number. A relational database could then connect the customer with the products, and you could then use the information from the resulting combined list. Paul Evers, a market research analyst, uses a relational database:

> I write, create and submit market research reports. I
> am commissioned by publishers of market research
> reports to produce reports in pharmaceutical and
> medical areas. These are hefty reports of about
> 200 – 250 pages. I do all the research, gather facts
> together, interpret them, speculate and forecast
> developments in a particular area over the next four or
> five years. The reports have six to seven chapters and
> an appendix.
>
> I use Access which is a relational database. I create a
> number of different databases and can input one

database into another. Each is stored in a different environment. If I have a compendium of facts and figures about different products plus a record of companies plus market sizes, I can, for example, relate the products to the companies or other markets.

Are databases easy to use?

Putting the information into a database is fairly straightforward so long as you are methodical and careful. The trouble comes when you have to retrieve information. At a basic level you can learn this easily. When you get on to more complicated things such as connecting or extracting information from two or more databases, then life becomes more complicated. You can learn by reading the manual. But Paul Evers warns:

The first time I used a database it was very difficult to get into the language. All applications – word processing, spreadsheets, graphics, databases – have their own jargon that you have to learn. But the instruction manuals are often badly written. They also make a misguided attempt to be user-friendly by repeating everything all the time.

☐ **If buying a new database, check how clear and informative the manual is.**

Denise Howells, a directory compiler, had her database set up for her:

Paradox is a database package which you can buy off the shelf. I had it especially designed, rewritten by a specialist who set up tables, cross-references and other things. It was set up for me how I wanted it so I found Paradox very easy to use.

> ☐ **You will find using your PC easier if you can get somebody to help you set up your PC and software for you. Find a local user's group and ask their advice.**

By far the quickest and best way to learn is to go on a training course so that you can see what to do and ask questions. Although, as Paul Evers says:

> On the few occasions I've tried training courses I've found them trying to be all things to all people. But my needs are specific to the business I'm in so I pick out what I need from the manual.

> ☐ **Check that any training course you plan to go on will deal with your specific computer needs.**

Using databases on a computer is acknowledged to be one of the more tricky aspects of computer work.

Because databases take up a lot of storage space and memory in a computer you do need to have as large a hard disk and as much RAM as possible.

COMPILING A DATABASE

This is straightforward. You will have or be given a typed list or other written information from which you must extract certain things, perhaps a name, address and phone number. You open the database and are taken through a series of instructions to help you name the fields, i.e. the names you are going to give each piece of information. So, in our example, you might call your fields NAME, ADDRESS, PHONE. The computer sets this on to a 'file card' on the screen and you can then type the information in, moving to a new file card for each new set of information.

If you are compiling a database for someone else you should make sure that you are quite clear about what information they want included. You do not want to get through a thousand records and then discover that your customer wants dates of birth added!

☐ **Make a list of the types of information to extract before you start.**

How to profit from a database

One obvious use of a database is to print labels or form letters using information in the database. You can feed a database into a compatible label printing or letter printing program. Mail merge packages use a database exclusively for the purpose of printing individually addressed form letters. (See Chapter 6 for more information about mail merge programs.)

You can use databases for compiling complicated brochures and information books. They can also be used to keep track of stock, sales, contacts and invoices for businesses.

Denise Howells used her database to compile her directory of business and consumer lists *Lists and Data Sources*:

I had the idea of setting up a directory listing all the

lists that were available everywhere in the UK into a single reference book. I had to write to everybody who I knew owned lists to send me all the details and then load them into the computer. Now it's an ongoing thing because the database is established and I update it twice a year.

Any kind of work where you need to extract information from large lists will benefit from databases. The information extracted can either be used on its own or used as a basis for further work using word processing or spreadsheets.

LEGAL PROBLEMS

You must be aware of the provisions of the Data Protection Act 1984. So long as you use a card file to keep information about individuals, there are no restrictions. Once the information is transferred to a computer then you have a duty to register yourself with the Office of Data Protection Register. This is 'to protect people from the misuse of personal information about them where that information is being processed by automatic means'. Under certain defined circumstances you must let people know that you hold information about them on your computer and give them a chance to have the information amended or removed. They are entitled to see a copy of any information that you hold on the computer about them.

There are certain rules for registration if you keep information in your database that includes personal data about living people – for example, names and addresses culled from an electoral roll. Anyone who is on your list has a right of access to the information about them. If your database contains a client list, mailing list, payroll, accounts or letters containing personal details then you may be liable for registration.

There are certain exemptions from both registration and subject access. You are exempt if you have personal data for calculating remuneration, pensions or keeping accounts; if your use is domestic; or if your data consists of the members' list of an unincorporated club whose members have given permission. You can use a list as a mailing list if it is for no other purpose and the subjects have given their consent.

You do not need to supply individuals with information on your list if you use it for statistics or research and the results will not enable individuals to be identified.

Text processing, e.g. writing a letter, is also exempt as long as it is not stored in any way.

If you are using or compiling a database containing personal details then get in touch with the Office for Data Protection Register and check whether you need to register with them.

If you do need to register then individuals on your list have the right of access to the information about them that you hold and can demand compensation for any inaccuracy or the loss or unauthorised disclosure of their details. They can demand that you correct or delete incorrect data.

Remember that when you compile or use a database it must:

- be obtained legally;
- be used for a lawful purpose;
- not be used for any other purpose than the original one;
- contain only the information needed for that purpose;
- be correct and up to date;
- be no longer than necessary;
- allow subject access;
- be subject to appropriate security.

You must check that any database you have on disk is used

subject to correct registration and procedures. It is notoriously difficult for people to find out who holds information about them, but that is no reason to abuse the Act.

WHAT WORK CAN YOU DO?

Your database may be useful in itself, for example a list of gardeners that might be of interest to garden equipment suppliers. So you could sell the lists on (see Chapter 6 for information about selling lists). There are a number of ways in which you can earn a living by using a database. You can:

- compile a database for a third party;
- insert a database into mail merge;
- create labels;
- address envelopes;
- sell copies of the list as disk, hard copy or labels;
- help compile bibliographies, catalogues etc.;
- conduct and store research for other people;
- maintain a subscription or membership list for publishers or clubs.

Using other databases

If you are doing research for someone or compiling a list for your own needs then you may need to extract information from other databases. If you are employed by a firm, you may be able to access a central company computer and extract information directly from it. Your employer should provide you with the necessary software to do this and you will also need a modem to connect your computer to the telephone. The software is called communications software and it reduces your files to the common computer language ASCII.

There are three main categories of on-line services – that is services you can connect to with your modem and PC. These are:

- extracting information from a controlled database;
- communications between individuals (E-mail);
- communication within a group which includes such things as bulletin boards.

Sending information to another computer in this way is called E-mail (electronic mail). If you are going to use this system for extracting information from other large databases, then you will need sophisticated software especially designed for information services.

Your modem should be one which can transmit your information quickly, otherwise you will run up huge phone bills. Ideally you should buy one that will run at the speed of faxes, that is 9,600 baud. (A baud is a way of describing the rate at which information can travel.) But one running at 2,400 baud would be usable.

You will need to pay for your phone calls, although these are usually charged at local rates. You will also need to pay the cost of joining an E-mail service such as BT Gold, CompuServe or CIX. Some of these offer conferencing and information services too. If you are extracting information from large databases then you will also pay a fee for each piece of information, such as an article, that you download (transfer to your computer).

If you work on your own then you may want to pay to join such a system. You will need a modem link for your phone and relevant software. Then you pay a rental fee to the organisation and pay for however much time you use in extracting information. You can also use this as an E-mail link, that is you can access the computers of other people on the same system and 'talk' to each other by leaving messages on their computer screens.

These systems can be expensive unless you are going to need regular access to different public databases.

Once you have a database and are using it you may need to buy software to help print out a database.

Many databases can print out well in a variety of forms, but some are inadequate. In the latter case you may want to improve the look of your database printout by buying a separate database publishing software such as Pagemaker Database Edition or Ventura Database Publisher. You may need this if you are compiling reports or directories and need to produce good copies.

EARNINGS

A specialist, such as a market research analyst, can charge a great deal. Paul Evers says:

> I work for myself supported by a few freelances who write individual chapters of a report. I pay myself half of my annual turnover. The difference is accounted for by paying for computers and software, buying the reference materials for my subject, paying the freelances, a part-time secretary, a photocopying machine and running a car (necessary in my business). You need to earn twice what you pay yourself.

You can charge per hour for compiling a database for a third party. Addressing envelopes and labels can be charged at so much per 1,000 plus a fixed fee.

Compiling and selling on specialist lists is even more lucrative. Many a large firm has discovered that their in-house compiled lists of customers' names and addresses can be sold to other companies for large sums of money.

6

MAIL MERGE AND DIRECT MAIL

WHEN YOU OPEN YOUR DAILY POST you will often find printed letters addressed to you personally. 'Ah, yes' you think, 'another form letter'. You can sometimes tell that a computer has printed in your name and perhaps your address by the way that it always seems to include your full name or initials as in 'Dear Mrs Joan Andrews'.

Someone, somewhere, produces these letters and arranges to post them. Large companies do this on a grand scale in-house or by farming out the work to specialist companies, but there is also a need for smaller operations. Small businesses or individuals often need to do personalised mailshots and cannot afford the larger firms. This is where you come in.

You can buy mail merge programs for PCs that will do this kind of work.

WHAT IS MAIL MERGE?

Mail merge is a type of software program that enables you to combine basic data, such as names and addresses, with information contained in a document such as a letter. So you can produce a basic letter or brochure and then the mail merge program will insert individual names. You can then print the original document with a different name or other information inserted for each copy.

A good mail merge program will guide you through the stages involved but there are three main steps to follow. You must:

- create a data file for the mail merge program to use (or you can in some programs use one you have already compiled);
- create a master document into which to insert the information from the database (or edit an existing document for this purpose);
- run the mail merge program so that the data is combined with the document and print the documents out.

The first thing you have to do is to create a data file. This is a set of records organised into different fields or pieces of information. So, if you are creating a data file of names and addresses, each name and address together is a record, and within the record the name is a field, the address is a field and so on. You can break down the fields to even smaller pieces of information such as a postcode or house name. (You will find more information about the uses to which you can put a data file or database in Chapter 5.)

Each field has to be given a name so, for example, the field name for the address might be ADDRESS.

You now create the data file by listing each record between record delimiters or symbols specified by your program that tell you where each record starts and stops. This list is then inserted into the data file under the different field names.

You then need to create or modify a document into which to insert the data. Everywhere you want to insert some original information, such as a name or address, you mark with a field name. Your program manual will tell you how. So everywhere in the document you want to insert an address you

60

would put the field name ADDRESS in our example. So perhaps a form letter would contain the fields: <NAME> <ADDRESS> <POSTCODE>.

When you are happy with the document you continue the merge program and it will then insert the individual names, addresses etc. into the documents ready for printing. You can usually look at the documents to check that the merge program has worked before you print anything.

WHAT SKILLS DO YOU NEED?

Patience is definitely a virtue in this business! It is not difficult to use a mail merge program and the instructions are usually straightforward. But you do need to be careful about creating the original document and accessing the correct sections of your database. Some mail merge programs allow you to create a database in the program to make connecting it to the main document easier.

Improve your chances of getting business by including in your services putting the documents in envelopes and posting them by a particular date. This is called a fulfilment service. Remember to include the cost of envelopes and postage in your fee. It takes time to stuff envelopes, and stick on stamps and address labels, so if you want to offer this service you may want to get a friend to help you for a fee or employ one of your family!

What Equipment Do You Need?

You will need a computer with as large a hard disk as possible, because your database and documents will take up a lot of space. You will need to decide what kind of printer will be suitable for your needs.

For simple letters sent out by an individual an ink jet printer might be all right. But for bulk printing out this will be rather slow. For this kind of bulk work you will need a laser printer, preferably a heavy-duty model, not only for speed but also for quality. If you are only going to be printing labels your printer will be working hard but a dot matrix printer would suffice.

Do not offer what you can't do. If you can produce basic text letters in black and white, offer those.

Direct Mail

Direct mail is another kind of use of a mail merge program. Direct mail is sending out literature or publications to a specified list of people. The contents need not be personalised mail, but the addresses on the envelopes or packets are. This kind of mail is the sort organisations use when contacting their members.

It involves similarly compiled databases but is concerned with producing such things as address labels or addressed envelopes. In fact, labels are more commonly used for direct mail by many firms because labels are less bulky to handle in large quantities and easier for printers to cope with. You can buy labels specially designed to be printed by computer printers.

With the appropriate software you can use a data file in a similar way. You define field names, and type in names and addresses as you would for mail merging. Then you can set out an envelope or label with the field positions marked. You can then run a mail merge, or label or an envelope addressing program to fill in individual names and addresses.

Equipment

Labels can be bought in sheets and put in the paper tray of a printer. Use the correct type of label for your printer. If you are going to do large quantities then you may want to buy a second paper tray if your printer can take one. For envelopes you will need an envelope tray/feeder if you are intending to print envelopes in bulk. Feeding envelopes in one at a time by hand is very slow and hardly cost-effective!

You can either offer to print labels and envelopes as a separate enterprise or combine it with producing personalised letters. Practise at home first to make sure that your envelope and label feed work properly and don't mangle the papers half-way through!

SUBSCRIPTION HANDLING

One kind of work which includes both maintaining a list and sending out mail to customers is subscription handling. This is becoming a growth area because subscriptions save publishers money. The more subscriptions publishers have the fewer copies they have to print for distributors and they don't have to pay a percentage to retailers. If you are interested in this kind of work you can also look for work from clubs or organisations.

For this work publishers or organisations pay you to maintain and operate their subscription lists. You have to keep the lists up to date, make sure that information about all new subscribers is added to the database and weed out people who no longer subscribe.

You also have to send out subscription reminders, invoices and sometimes back copies, although some people just maintain the lists. If you do send out copies they have to be sent out on time and you will need adequate, dry storage space.

You will get subscribers phoning you up with questions and complaints which makes for a lot of extra work. You will also have to pay the subscription money into the bank. You may find it can get very boring typing in lots of names. There will be mail to keep track of as well as money, so anyone doing this work has to be efficient. When the monthly deadlines are near things can get very busy.

You will need a PC with a large memory because your lists will take up a lot of room and you will need to have room for adding more. Ideally you should have a laser printer because the work involves a lot of printing, especially labels. But people do operate lists with good-quality dot matrix printers. You will need a database program, a word processing program with mail merge and separate label printing software. You won't need much stationery but you may want to have a leaflet printed professionally to send out to prospective clients.

If you do mailouts you will have to get a franking machine and a sealing machine for the regular supplies of polythene mailing bags. Most magazines are sent in plastic covers nowadays. You will also have to register with the Data Protection Register.

Selling Lists

It is possible to earn money from the lists themselves. You can either sell these lists, or part of them, on to other people or you can use them to arrange direct mailshots for other people.

Lists can be compiled from directories, telephone enquiries, replies to advertisements, questionnaires, personal visits, electoral registers and so on. But as Carrie Colliss, marketing manager for Merlin Publications, says:

> How you obtain the names for your list will depend on what sort of list you want. You could have a list of people that buy books, or who are interested in business opportunities, or who are interested in reading magazines – absolutely anything. In order to get those sorts of people you need to advertise and offer them something in an area where those kinds of people are going to be reading it.

You could spend time compiling lists and then sell your lists on, but it is probably more time-efficient to act as a manager for another list owner and administer the sale or rental of their lists. Brokers also supply lists but act on behalf of the users. Carrie Colliss says:

> All publishers rent out their lists now unless it's for a new subscription interest magazine. Then they might want to keep it for a while and use it themselves before they sell or rent it on to someone else. You can get lists of practically anything now. Someone could buy a list and use it to sell on. Obviously you'd have to agree arrangements.

Publishers use list managers to help them get some revenue

from their lists. Carrie Colliss suggests this as a way of making money:

> You could go to a publisher of a very specialist magazine. They might not have the time or facilities to rent out those names or addresses but they want to bring the revenue. So you may be like a list broker. You would sell that list on their behalf and take a 20 per cent commission on each list that you rent out.

Lists are often advertised in trade journals and you can sometimes spot ads for list managers.

Your customers will be people who want to send out a mailing themselves, and need a certain number of names and addresses.

There are several ways you can sell a list on:

● single rental – the customer can use the list once only;
● outright purchase – the customer buys the list but cannot resell it;
● gross billing – you sell the customer the whole list but do not adjust the price for any names not used;
● net names – the customer pays only for names used. You give a reduction for unusable names of up to 15 per cent of the fee.

You will need to be able to extract certain types of information for different customers. So for one customer you might need to supply the names of all the people living in one county or for another everyone in the ABC social class range. You will be able to do that with your computer list used on a database.

WHAT EQUIPMENT DO YOU NEED?

Because selling or renting lists depends on compiling and maintaining large databases you will need a sophisticated PC with lots of memory, as well as the appropriate software. Carrie Colliss advises:

If you want to set up doing this in your home you need a sophisticated computer system. You need to be able to database names and addresses, and have fields that represent other information such as 'this person enquired but they haven't bought'. Otherwise the only way you could select from your list would be by postcode or you do what's called an nth selection. That is, for example, where you take every sixteenth name. There's special database marketing software. You need a good dot matrix printer to be able to do the labels.

Problems of size

In order to offer a viable service providing mailing lists you will need to have a database with a minimum of four to five thousand names on it, preferably more. The time-consuming part of the work is keying in the large amounts of data.

☐ **It is possible to do this on your own if you administer a small, specialised list but you will probably find that you will need to employ one or two helpers to key in the data for you while you administer the lists.**

Carrie Colliss has this advice for home operators:

> You need to have a minimum of 4,000 to 5,000 names
> on a mailing list to have anything that's worth selling
> to anybody because you want to be able to do
> selections. It depends on what your database is going
> to be. We've got 200,000 items and I wouldn't test
> probably less than 4,000 or 5,000. People do want to
> test less but it's really not a big enough sample testing
> 500 or 1,000 from a database. If you send out 500
> you might get one response and people think 'Oh
> that's not very good'. If you're getting a response rate
> of 1 to 2 per cent in the industry as a whole then
> you're doing quite well.

You can buy specialised software for database marketing, and
organisations such as the Direct Marketing Association will
give advice. You may have had experience of this kind of
work in the course of previous employment, but if not then
there are courses that will teach you the work.

WHAT JOBS CAN YOU DO?

You can sell your lists to people in a number of different
forms:

- as pre-printed labels;
- on disk in a language compatible with the customer's own
  WP;
- as a printed list (a 'hard copy') with or without pre-printed
  labels;
- as pre-printed envelopes.

You should aim to turn any orders round in two to three days.

Fulfilment service

If you like you can include a 'fulfilment' service which means that you take the customer's mail and stuff the envelopes, frank the envelopes and distribute them. On a small scale you can stick stamps on, but for large orders you will need to get a franking machine from the Post Office or arrange to bundle envelopes for bulk franking by the Post Office. If you have a minimum of 500 identical letters they will waive the 3 per cent surcharge. If you are sending at least 4,000 items and will sort them by postcode you can get discounts of between 8 and 32 per cent on postage costs. Look under 'Royal Mail' in the telephone directory for where to apply. You charge for a fulfilment service per 1,000 envelopes.

Franking machines

If you want to provide the complete fulfilment service then you will need to get a franking machine. These print a form of postage stamp on to an envelope. You pay an amount to the Post Office in advance and the franking machine's meter is set to that amount. When each envelope is stamped the machine deducts the price of a stamp from its meter until it reaches zero. At this point the machine locks. Franked mail has to be handed in at a Post Office.

It is possible to get electronic franking machines that are obviously much more expensive. But they can include such extra features as recording the value and number of items in one batch, printing out postage costs, or interfacing with some electronic scales so that when a letter is weighed and the destination keyed in the franking machine automatically calculates the postage amount and sets the meter for this. Franking machines can be used for parcels as well, but you are not likely to want to deal with this kind of bulky mail from your sitting room!

WHERE TO FIND WORK

Your customers are likely to be small local businesses or individuals working from home. You can print a one-page leaflet, and deliver it to local shops and business premises. Advertise in the local paper, particularly in the business section or supplement. Local clubs, organisations and societies may want you to send out information to their members. Large institutions or businesses often have their own mail merge facilities.

You can advertise your lists in the small ads of magazines like *Marketing* or *Marketing Week. The Publishing Magazine* is useful if you are interested in subscription handling work. Send leaflets or put cards through the doors of local businesses. Schools and colleges might offer you work for special mailings.

EARNINGS

You charge per 1,000 addresses or pieces of information. Adjust your charges according to your market.

In addition to your basic charge you can charge 'selection' or 'extraction' fees for selecting addresses according to particular criteria such as a certain geographical area or age range. Carrie Colliss says:

You have to work out your prices whether you're actually selling or renting. If you sell then you've lost your rights to it, and the buyer has bought it outright and can sell it on again. If you sell outright then you should delete those names from your list. But if you rent it then you rent it for a 'one time only' use so you put in sleeper names to find out if they've used it again without your authorisation.

Sleeper names are false names inserted into your list. They have your address so that you can tell when the list is being used. For doing a count of the number of addresses in a particular group you would not charge anything and would expect to give the answer within a day.

If, instead of addresses only, your customer wants to buy personal names for personalised letters then you can charge extra. You can also charge extra for each number of mailshots your customer wants to use the list for.

7

SPREADSHEETS

A SPREADSHEET is a common second PC program because it is number based and so is a natural addition to a word processing program. If your PC came with a business software 'bundle' of programs you will probably have a spreadsheet program, even if you haven't yet used it. Now that information technology (IT) is taught in schools even children have some understanding of the use of spreadsheets. So if they can learn how to use them, you can too!

Spreadsheets are commonly used for accountancy or forecasting work. As well as making bookkeeping and accountancy easier they can also be used for making calculations, analysis, forecasting and producing charts from given figures.

It is possible to buy separate bookkeeping and accountancy packages if you just want to do basic accounts and many small businesses do indeed use them for just that. You may be using a basic home accounts package to keep track of your family's income and expenditure. But for anything more complicated a spreadsheet package is better.

If you have spreadsheet software already installed on your PC, you will need to learn about its more complicated functions. You can use it to offer bookkeeping, accounting or forecasting services to other people.

An additional advantage is that it will help you to keep accurate business records, which is very important for any home business. Therefore, using your accountancy packages or spreadsheets for keeping your own accounts in order will be a bonus. This will not in itself help you make money from your computer, but it will make your home computer business more efficient and reliable. With your own accounts in order you will have more time to concentrate on the money-making advantages of the spreadsheet package.

WHAT IS A SPREADSHEET?

A spreadsheet is basically a large, two-dimensional table divided into sections or cells into which you can type information. For example, in the table below, one cell might be defined as row 2, column E. This table can be of almost unlimited size, even though all of it may not be visible on the screen at any one time. Headings can be put at the top of columns and at the side of rows to make keying in the information easier.

Spreadsheets are used for compiling tables of figures which can then be used as the basis of calculations that the spreadsheet program can perform. A good spreadsheet package can deal in numbers, text and dates equally well.

	A	B	C	D	E	F	G
1			Income	Expense	PROFIT OR LOSS		
2	Jones		£300.00	£237.00	£63.00		
3	Smith		£240.00	£265.00	£25.00		
4	Brown		£431.00	£341.00	£90.00		
5	TOTAL				£178.00		

In one column you might list a set of particulars, for example, names of suppliers, and in the rows you might list income and expenditure or other sets of figures.

You could then ask the program to calculate totals or other numerical information and put the answer in another cell. To do this you need to put in a formula that will make these calculations. Spreadsheet programs usually include some of the more useful formulae. You can ask the program to make calculations automatically when you alter details in the spreadsheet. So, for example, if you altered the rate of exchange when calculating foreign income you could get the spreadsheet to reflect changed totals automatically.

You can also ask the program to make calculations in order to make forecasts. So you might ask it to calculate a year's sales figures using one month's figures as a basis. The program will not only produce figures, but also change these into charts and graphs if necessary. One Windows-based spreadsheet program Excel can even simulate 3-D charts. You could create different tables for each month and a summary chart at the end of the year, for example. You can also use spreadsheets as a basic database, but this is a waste of such a program's capabilities.

Spreadsheets can import information from other databases.

Charts and graphs

Producing charts and graphs is an important part of a spreadsheet's use. These make numerical information more accessible to the average person than pages of figures or tables of numbers. They can be in the form of bar or column charts (as shown), pie charts or graphs. Most good spreadsheet programs will allow you to choose from a number of graph and chart types.

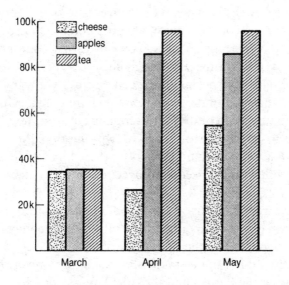

Well-known spreadsheet programs include Microsoft Excel and Lotus 1-2-3. Shareware companies often sell cheap and easier-to-use spreadsheet and accountancy packages.

WHAT SKILLS WILL YOU NEED?

Certainly you need to be numerate. Although using a spreadsheet on a computer makes calculations easier, the work will only be as accurate as the information put into the machine. You need to be able to tell when an answer or forecast is inaccurate enough to make it likely that incorrect figures have been put in, or that a formula has been incorrectly inserted. You should at least not be afraid of numbers and be prepared to learn.

If you intend to offer accountancy, bookkeeping or

forecasting services then you should have some kind of training. Adult education colleges commonly offer bookkeeping courses as do distance learning colleges. You can learn accountancy at college full or part time. Clients giving you any kind of work involving figures, especially financial figures, will want to be reassured that you understand what you are doing. Miscalculating numbers can be disastrous for any business. It will also help you to attract customers if your promotional literature can say that you are qualified to offer these kinds of financial services. John Mills, a self-employed accountant, says:

> The larger firms use me to produce market forecasts and management accounts. Lots of large companies have people to put the figures into the spreadsheet but they often don't understand what the figures mean. I can check the figures and the calculations, and do more complicated calculations for them. Because I understand how spreadsheets work, as well as being trained in accountancy, I can see where the program is producing incorrect figures because of badly programmed calculations. This can save firms a great deal of money.
>
> I am a qualified accountant and I do think that you must have some training before offering this kind of service to the public.

You need to be accurate because the basis of all the results produced by the spreadsheet will be the accuracy of the figures and formulae put into it. You also need to spend some time learning how to use a spreadsheet package. It is not the easiest of software to use, although you can teach yourself by following the manual carefully. Like database packages it is worth getting some instruction and hands-on experience before trying it on your own. If you have training in accountancy or spreadsheet work, or have done similar work in a full-time job then you will be at an advantage.

What Can You Do?

You can:

- do accounting work for firms and individuals;
- produce forecasting reports;
- do bookkeeping;
- do record keeping;
- do management accounts;
- compile statistics;
- produce financial appraisals;
- become a financial consultant.

What kind of work you choose to do will depend on your own expertise and what you think you can learn. You can choose to work for small local firms or offer your expertise to larger companies as John Mills does:

I work for a number of individuals and small local businesses on a regular basis, but my clients also include one or two larger firms further afield. For the large firms I provide forecasts and financial reports.

Lots of local businesses – my local newsagent and even the local music shop spring to mind – have their own computers, and specially modified software for stock control and accounts. However they still need someone to produce regular financial reports and to do the detailed accounting for their annual tax returns. Individuals employ me to do their bookkeeping.

This kind of work is not something you can offer unless you are confident that you are good at it. No one will thank you for producing inaccurate figures.

WHERE CAN YOU GET WORK?

Advertise in business magazines or management magazines. Contact local businesses and shops. Send out leaflets to larger firms. Try advertising in specialist magazines where you might attract customers who run a business based on their hobby.

☐ **The local press may run a special business page or insert which will come to the notice of local firms.**

EARNINGS

You do need some training in bookkeeping or record keeping to offer those skills and be qualified if you are offering accountancy services. If you are a qualified accountant you can charge high fees for your services but remember that this may price you out of the market if you expect to cater for small local businesses and individuals.

8

CASH FROM BUSINESS GRAPHICS

PRESENTATIONS LOOM LARGE in the world of business and have engendered their own specifically designed software called business graphics. This is for business users who need to create documents for presentations and want to have all the necessary software in one easy-to-use package. Using business graphics software on your PC can help you make money.

It is possible for anyone who applies themselves to learning how to use their PC and the programs on it to produce adequate-looking work with efficient word processing software, and perhaps, for the more advanced users, desktop publishing (DTP) software. But a business graphics package makes good-looking business documents straightforward to produce and within the range of any competent user. After all they are designed for use by anyone in a large company from the managing director down.

The title 'presentation work' has a double meaning too. Not only is this chapter about documents prepared for presentations, that is, the conferences, seminars and talks of business life, but the documents must also look good. In other words documents for presentations must be well presented.

What is Presentation Work?

At conferences, seminars and in boardrooms all over the UK every day people are standing up in front of others and giving a talk about their work. It may involve showing slides or overheads (text and diagrams on acetate sheets that can be projected on to a screen), commenting on a report, supporting a proposal or discussing a forecast.

Each of these things – overheads, report, proposal, forecast – has to be presented not only orally but by a printed package that is elegant and easy to read. The production of these is a job you can do with your computer.

So presentation work involves producing the material that supports oral presentations, and producing it in a way that enhances the talk or discussion and looks good in its own right. To do this you can use a business graphics package.

What is Business Graphics?

Because presentation work is so important in business software companies have produced special programs that contain all the items necessary to produce a good-looking document or overhead. Typically a package will include templates of different designs for presentation documents and overheads, and the capabilities to create charts and diagrams, include pictures and add headers and footers. They will enable you to import graphs, charts and graphics from other programs as well. There is usually a limited choice of document design but the format is made as easy as possible to use. There are pages designed for title page, bullet point chart, data pages for charts and graphs and flow charts, and diagram trees as well as pages for text. Examples include Lotus Freelance Graphics or Microsoft's Harvard Graphics. You simply choose the most effective version for the job and fill in the client's information. The information can be inserted into predesignated areas or frames in the document.

The programs include covers and inside sheets in various designs for the longer documents, and sets type and style of overhead sheets so that you do not have to worry about whether the text can be read when you project the overhead.

WHAT SKILLS DO YOU NEED?

Obviously, if you concentrate on presentation work you will need keyboard skills and be able to use a business graphics package. This is straightforward to learn if you follow the tutorial in your manual, but you need to practise before you offer your work commercially.

If you have research skills you may add these to your presentation skills and write the report as well as produce it, as do Louise Samuel, a market researcher, and her colleague:

> I write sections of the final report. I interview drug companies and talk to pharmacies and end users. This is industrial research rather than consumer research. I have to find out what the sales of drugs are, what the costs are, future pricing, market trends and so on.
> Then I have to write up the results.
> Using the computer makes it easy for me to

incorporate secondary information from specialists, for example. I send my work to my associate who edits it and adds the forecasts. Some reports are edited by clients themselves. We do other reports together and my boss produces the reports using desktop publishing software, then he arranges for the printing and covers.

If you cannot do all of this you can simply provide a service for producing the documents in a form suitable for presentation.

You will also need to be able to draw up graphs and charts from given data, and be able to present a well thought out, good-looking document.

Documents needing more complicated design work will need desktop publishing programs and skills. Although these can be and are applied to presentation work it is possible to produce good work without them and at a competitive price. There is more about this in Chapter 9. As far as presentation work is concerned I am assuming you need to provide text with diagrams and charts inserted, and for which you can use business graphics programs and your word processing skills. For overheads, you will need to produce clear diagrams and words on acetate.

Of course most large organisations do all these things in-house. Even directors have been known to produce their own overheads. But smaller organisations or individuals without the time or money to spare may well need your help.

WHAT EQUIPMENT WILL YOU NEED?

You will need a printer capable of taking acetate sheets for producing overhead slides. Check with your printer's manual to see if yours can do that. However, be aware that acetate sheets do tend to get mangled in a computer's printer.

> ☐ **Professionals produce the overhead design on their computer, print out a plain paper copy and then photocopy this on to the acetate. This often produces a better result in any case.**

Your software should be able to collate multiple documents so that instead of printing out all the page ones, and all the page twos, it prints a whole document in page order, then the next one.

If you are producing the finished report you will need binders and possibly a binding machine. These can be either plastic comb binding, thermal heaters which secure the pages like a paperback book, plastic slips that slide over the spines or even nice folders. They can be bought from large office suppliers such as Office World or Rymans. Find out what your client wants and is prepared to pay for before you go ahead and take the job. Staples will not do, except for internal reports and documents specified by your client. They are, in any case, less suitable for bulky documents.

You will need to produce charts and graphs, so make sure the business graphics package you use can either do this or will allow you to import these from other programs. Some word processing programs can produce these in a simplified form.

Overheads can be done on word processing software, but it is quicker and more effective to use business graphics software specially designed for presentation work.

Design

As far as design goes you will need to have a good idea of how a well laid out report should look. A business graphics package does the work for you. For long reports you will need to use footnotes, headers and footers, page numbering, line numbering, indexing, contents making etc. Does your word processing software do this? DTP software is probably unnecessary unless the report is intended for commercial publication. You may need a scanner to include pictures in the documents if the report consists of illustrations as well as text. But business graphics programs typically include a number of standard illustrations such as maps, arrows, boxes and pictures of office equipment.

REPORTS

Reports range from 10 copies of a simple 5-page document for the directors' eyes only to a massive 100-page tome for an entire sales force. It will give information about the progress of the business or part of it, and will probably include figures, charts and graphs as well as text.

Find out from your clients how many copies they want, what quality paper is needed, how it should be bound and what logo, if any, should be incorporated on the cover. Does your client want a plain paper cover, or card or plastic? Is only one unbound copy required for commercial or internal printing, or are you expected to produce all the copies? What is the deadline?

Many firms will have a set format for reports. If you can see a better way of setting them out discuss it with the client. They may be pleased to see a better and perhaps more cost- effective way of doing things.

Even a small firm will have a business heading or logo and by using a scanner you can incorporate this into the front cover design, along with the title and the date of the report.

CONFERENCE DOCUMENTS

Conference reports can be of two types: either a document containing information to be read before the conference; or a collection of the speeches made at the conference to be sent to all participants and interested parties afterwards. You may have to produce the latter in sections if speakers delay sending copies of their speeches to the organisers.

Make sure you understand whether the conference organiser will send you all the speeches together or whether the speakers will send copies directly to you. If they are to be sent directly agree with the organiser who is responsible for chasing up the latecomers. Unless you want to offer editing services make sure that the organiser understands that all speeches will be produced as written apart from a standard spell check. This is particularly important where the subject is a specialist one using jargon or technical terms you are not familiar with.

PRESENTATIONS

The documents needed for presentations are similar to reports. The difference is that while a report may be for circulation and private reading, a presentation document is supporting a talk or discussion. Commonly this talk is on an aspect of someone's job or a discussion of methods and future action.

Again the document may be simply a few pages or a large bulky document. Similar criteria apply. The deadline may be tighter than for reports because the person giving the presentation will need to read it and it may need to be sent to participants ahead of time.

OVERHEADS

Overheads are text and pictures used in overhead projectors. They are produced on acetate sheets and lit in such a way as to throw the image on to a wall or screen. They are popular with speakers, and are less expensive and easier to use than slides and slide projectors.

Overheads need to be clear and uncluttered. The lettering you use needs to be simple and of large enough size to be easily read when projected. Diagrams, too, must be uncluttered and easy to read.

If you are working from someone's notes ask for clarification of any unclear words or figures. You don't want the word 'Elephant' to flash on to the screen when the speaker meant 'Blueprint'. There would be a lot of questions from the audience!

You can design overheads using a word processor and adding diagrams by hand after printing. However, this looks unprofessional and nowadays there is plenty of business graphics software available which can produce everything you need on screen for printing.

☐ **If there is time, supply a copy of the overhead in draft on plain paper for the originator to check before producing the final version.**

In any case, you should always supply a plain paper printout of the overhead as well as the acetate sheet. This is because speakers refer to these and use them to separate the overheads from each other when stored in a pile.

You can limit your work with overheads to producing the overhead from a completed file on disk or final hard copy supplied by the client, rather than designing it from a rough draft.

WHERE TO FIND WORK

Your obvious hunting ground for presentation work is businesses with a large enough work force to make presenting reports likely. You can also offer to produce overheads and proposals for individuals who will be going to conferences. Stress in your advertising that you can produce as many copies as required, and that making alterations for different types of jobs and firms is a quick and easy process.

EARNINGS

Keep the information on a disk so that you can run off more copies and make alterations if the client comes back for more.

For producing overheads you can charge a fee per item if the customer supplies their own files on disk for you to work with. If you are going to offer to work in this way then you need to have file conversion facilities in your software so that you can use any kind of files from any program. These programs are advertised in PC magazines. For producing overheads from hard copy supplied by the customer you can charge more.

If the customer gives you a rough draft and asks you to work from it to produce the overhead then obviously you charge more.

The cost of reports and presentation documents will depend on the size of the document, how many copies are required and how complicated it is.

9

DESKTOP
PUBLISHING

DESKTOP PUBLISHING (DTP) is a glamorous but misleading term. The immediate assumption is that it means you can produce a book from typescript to bound copy on your desk at home using a computer. Although this *is* possible (and requires a lot more equipment than most people will have sitting around at home), it usually means the processes that lead to a printer being able to produce the final copies. But you can use DTP to produce all kinds of documents for other people.

DTP is using a computer and a printer to combine words and pictures to produce high-quality hard copy that looks as near as possible like a commercially printed product. It is commonly applied to almost any system that includes typesetting, well-designed layouts, and often graphics and scanned photographic images. You can produce simple leaflets and brochures from start to finish like this, but in the case of books or magazines then the process needs to be finished by a printer. You can do the preliminary stages on your computer and save yourself or your clients money.

Directory compiler, Denise Howells, says using DTP saves a lot of money:

I used to pay £2,000 twice a year to have the directory

typeset. But now I do all the typesetting myself with DTP. So I save myself £4,000 a year on that alone.

What is DTP For?

As DTP replaces the traditional printing process it will be helpful to explain what this is. The publisher receives a typescript which is edited and then marked up to show the styles and kinds of type to be used. The typescript is then retyped using a typesetting machine according to the specifications and the result is printed on to long sheets called galleys. The text is then the correct type and width. When these galleys have been proof-read (that is say corrections are made to the text), the corrected text is then printed on to photographic paper as printed pages. These are then pasted on to board together with any illustrations. At this stage it is called camera ready copy (CRC). These are then photographed and used by a printer to make plates from which to produce the finished work.

A computer can help to eliminate many of the preliminary stages leading to CRC, and to make the process easier and quicker. Text is typed on to a screen either directly into a DTP program or by importing it from a word processing program. Instructions can be given to alter the text and size of page on the screen until it is exactly how it will appear in the book. DTP programs operate WYSIWYG (pronounced 'wizzywig') which means 'What you see is what you get', so you can see exactly what the page will look like with the type shown exactly as it will be printed. You can see what happens when you make each change and immediately see how the finished result will look.

Footnotes, page numbers, and headings and footers can be

added easily and automatically. A draft copy can be quickly printed out for proof-reading and any changes made immediately and viewed on the screen.

A final copy can be printed on a laser printer. For small runs this is adequate in itself. For longer runs it can then be used by a printer as CRC for photocopying or to be photographed for plate-making for the conventional printing process.

For top-quality reproduction the CRC can be produced on a special version of a typesetting machine which can take files directly from desktop publishing programs.

☐ **Don't run off lots of colour prints on your printer. It is uneconomical for more than a few copies. You will need to take your design to a printer, but in that case you should provide colour separation sheets – separate sheets of the design in the four colours used by printers – magenta, cyan, yellow and black. You can then have as many colour copies as you like at an inexpensive price and better quality. (See also page 112.)**

Jessica Beveridge, a graphic designer, says:

You can make mistakes with printers as far as colour is concerned. People tend to think that you've got this colour thing on your screen and you just print it out on a colour printer. The problem is that it's an extremely expensive method of producing colour for volume. You have to create colour separations. People make it look pretty on the screen and then don't realise that to get something out of a colour printer is going to be costing them £1.50 a page which is just not economical if you want more than about 10 or 20 copies.

Computer-aided design

Computer-aided design or CAD refers to specially dedicated programs that are meant for use by people with a scientific or technical background. They consist of the shapes, symbols and special curves such as Bezier curves necessary to produce such things as house plans, technical drawings or circuit designs. They can produce overlapping layers and some programs can design in 3-D. Unless you have training in one of these areas these programs are best left to experts. If you are familiar with this kind of work then such programs can make producing such designs much easier.

EQUIPMENT

Some of the more powerful word processing programs are capable of some of the things a DTP program can do, and can produce good quality leaflets, simple newsletters and reports. They often include templates or style sheets for these. But DTP programs have more features which enable fine manipulating of text and graphics, and can cope with very complex documents and long works such as books.

You can get DTP programs for most machines. They do take up a lot of memory in the computer so make sure that your computer can cope with particular programs. The best known DTP programs for PCs are Aldus Pagemaker, Corel Ventura Publisher and Quark Xpress. These will cope with books as well as smaller publications. A mid-range program with fewer facilities is Deskpress. More basic, cheaper programs are Timeworks Desktop Publisher, Microsoft Publisher and Serif Page Plus. Mac users have their own version of Pagemaker and Quark Xpress, and there are DTP programs for Acorn, Amiga and Atari users.

However, there are cheaper shareware programs that can do many of the things that the major programs can do.

Almost all DTP programs use text and graphics files stored on disks. They can be produced in the DTP programs themselves, but the quality is usually better if they are imported from dedicated word processing or graphics programs.

You must have the Windows environment, as described in Chapter 1, to use these programs. Try to find a program that lets text flow from one page to another as required, as well as flowing round pictures. It should be able to produce multiple columns on the page, have a wide variety of fonts which can be printed at any size, and support manual and automatic kerning. Kerning means adjusting the position of letters to improve how the text looks. It is particularly useful for certain pairs of letters such as 'AV' (to avoid the eye being distracted by too much white space between them) and is more usually applied to headings.

It need not cost much to set up in DTP. Denise Howells says:

> Really the overheads are very small. I've updated my
> computer and got a snazzier laser printer and a new
> fax machine, but that's all really. Obviously you have
> to buy the software.

If you decide to start DTP then decide what you aim to do. Are you going to produce leaflets and brochures for your clients? Or are you going to offer professional DTP services for magazine and book publishers? Denise advises:

> If you're setting up publishing on your own at home,
> make sure it's to do something you know about.

If you have no training in DTP or design then you may be content to produce leaflets and brochures, reports and mailshots. Check what your word processing program can do.

Some of the more sophisticated WP programs are perfectly capable of producing elegant leaflets and newsletters. But if you want to branch out beyond that then you will need to spend money on a more sophisticated separate DTP package. This could cost you several hundred pounds.

Printers

Your printer will be a very important part of your DTP service. For simple leaflets or basic newsletters you can use an ink jet printer, but these are slow and although the quality is very good it is not quite up to laser printer standard. If you have an ink-jet printer forget books and more sophisticated magazines until you can afford a laser printer.

☐ **Don't bother with a colour printer unless it will be vital to your work. Low-resolution colour printers are inadequate for decent DTP. If most of your work will be with black and white pictures or text only then go for a top-class mono laser printer if you are thinking of buying a new one.**

Scanners

Unless you are going to confine your DTP work to text only or to pictures drawn on the PC in a drawing program you will need to buy a scanner. These are machines that will 'read' pictures and feed them into your DTP program so that they can be altered and moved around to fit the text. You can buy a hand-held one to start with, but in the long run a 'flat bed' scanner which can scan a whole page at once will be more useful.

You can do without a scanner, by pasting pictures into the pages of text by hand before a printer reproduces them.

Photographs must be professionally scanned before being pasted because they cannot be reproduced unless they are broken up into a series of dots of different shades of grey (look closely at pictures in newspapers).

Once you have the text and pictures in your DTP program, you can either print them out or give your disk to a service bureau to print out high-quality copies of the pages for you.

YOU REALLY WANT TO PRODUCE BOOKS?

It is now possible to produce an entire book yourself – or at least an A5 paperback – entirely on your kitchen table. But the cost of setting up with the necessary equipment could cost you thousands of pounds. Unless you have a great deal of time, are a brilliant publicist and can afford to invest a lot of money before breaking even this is hardly going to make you a millionaire. For those who like the sound of this a firm called Book-Builder (see 'Useful addresses' at the back of this book) will supply you with all the necessary equipment (or parts thereof) and software to enable you to produce a book from start to finish.

You will need a main computer and perhaps a second 'slave' computer connected to it to operate the printing program if you need to do other work on your main PC at the same time. You will also need a high-quality printer, a guillotine, a thermal binder and dedicated software. The cost of a complete system can range from just under £4,000 to nearly £40,000! Unless you don't need to earn much money and have loads of cash to spare concentrate on the usual DTP process.

WHAT ELSE DO YOU NEED?

It is possible to teach yourself to use a DTP program but desktop publishing is not simply the combining of text and pictures on a page and printing it out. Unless the whole design of the page is satisfactory it can look cheap and be ineffective.

DTP involves design as much as the technicalities of putting the page together. What style and size of type will you use? How many pictures? How will the page be arranged? How much white space should you leave? How do you put a double spread together so that it looks pleasant?

A well-designed document should lead your eye through the page to the points that need to be got across. This needs to be done in order. It has to be done in a sensible but attractive way.

There are two different parts to DTP – page layout and graphic design. Page layout is a more involved form of word processing and can be tackled by anyone who is prepared to learn the basics of DTP. Graphic designer, Jessica Beveridge, has firm views on this:

> If you are doing basic DTP where the graphic design has been done by somebody else and you're essentially following a template, anybody who can use a computer can do it. The major problem with DTP is that most people don't realise that they actually need to know quite a lot of design to be able to produce a document which is going to convey information properly.

Jessica warns you not to overlook the design element:

> There are two things about graphic design. One is that no matter how much you learn, some people just

cannot see when a page looks well balanced and other people can. There is an artistic element in it.

The second point is that people also tend not to know anything actually about the basic principles of design, which is why what most people produce when they get hold of a DTP package uses everything all over the place. The result is something that does not actually transmit the information that you want to transmit in your publication.

☐ **Take Jessica's advice and try to get some training and hands-on experience before you start to offer your work commercially.**

If you already have training in design, graphics or typography then you may well find it easier to get to work. But before you advertise your services make sure that you can produce a well put together product on time.

Practise by producing work for free – perhaps your school or club needs a small poster or leaflet, or your society newsletter needs redesigning. Have a go until you are confident of producing professional-quality work.

Many DTP and WP programs include style sheets for various kinds of documents including leaflets and newsletters. You can start by using these as a basis for your work until you have the confidence to alter them for your own or your clients' needs.

Jessica has this to say about training in desktop publishing:

I do desktop publishing as part of my work. Clients can send me work in the post on a disk and I take the word processed stuff, turn it into laid-out pages and design all the covers.

If people use a template they can manage but there

is more to it than meets the eye. You've got to get training or you've got to put a lot of work into learning it. You're not going to get work from people if what you produce is a horrible mess. You may think it looks wonderful but you're not going to make a commercial success of it.

Typography

You need to think carefully about the look of your text. There are many good books on the subject but basically you need to know how and when to use kerning, line spacing (leading) and something about different type sizes and styles (fonts). One good rule is not to use more than two styles of type, but alter the look of the page by using bold, or italics and altering the type size. How you range the type on the page is an art in itself.

WHAT WORK CAN YOU DO?

Consider the following possibilities:

- leaflets;
- price lists;
- brochures;
- catalogues;
- posters;
- directories;
- forms;
- advertisements;
- booklets;
- layout for books and magazines;
- newsletters.

Even if your customers will have the pages printed commercially they can save money by asking you to do the layout for them.

WHERE TO FIND WORK

Advertise your expertise with your own leaflet. Use this to show off your skill so make sure that it is well designed, clear, effective and interesting. Send it to local businesses, local societies and clubs, and take out small ads in writers' magazines.

If you feel you can make it work you could start your own newsletter or magazine. You will need to ask local firms to advertise and to guarantee distribution (can you really deliver 5,000 copies or more all by yourself every week or month?). See if there is a need for a newspaper in your area. Successful magazines and local papers have been started with two pages, cheaply produced and sold in local newsagents. If they can do it you can. But you will need a lot of energy and willingness to sell yourself to make it work.

EARNINGS

Your earnings from DTP will depend on the type of work you are offering and how experienced you are. Obviously a trained designer with years of experience who can produce four-colour separations and design full-length books or magazines will be able to charge more than someone who is simply offering to design letterheads or simple leaflets. Phone up a few local businesses and ask what they are charged for the services you want to offer and then pitch your price a little lower.

10

PUBLICITY WORK

AN OVERLOOKED AREA of home computer work is publicity. Think of all the people out there who have a small business or who have started working from home. Unlike the larger companies they cannot afford to employ a professional public relations officer or pay for expensive advertising, but they still need to get their service or goods known to the public. This is where you can come in.

Instead of producing work to sell on your computer and publicising your services why not use your computer to help other businesses publicise theirs?

PUBLICITY OR ADVERTISING?

Note that I am suggesting you should consider offering publicity as a money-making scheme for your PC, not offering to arrange your customers' advertising. When advertisements appear in the media they are paid for by the business concerned. Publicity, on the other hand, is the free mention of the business, product or service in the media. In many ways this is more valuable, because whereas advertising is what the company says about itself, publicity is perceived to be what other people say about the company and is expected to be less biased. (This is not always the case, of course!)

You will be charging people to arrange for information about their business to be sent to the media in such a form as might prompt the media to make some mention of the business. The result might be, for example, an article, photograph or radio interview featuring the business or your client.

What Can You Do?

There are many ways in which you can use your computer to help other people with their publicity. You can write and produce news releases, leaflets and small posters, and mail these to the relevant media. You can encourage people to write to the press, and type and send their letters. You can set out and send sales letters, news-sheets and brochures.

What Skills Do You Need?

You should be able to set out, type and print documents. Some awareness of good leaflet design would be useful. But most of all you will need a head for a good news snippet.

You may simply be asked to set out and print publicity material that someone in the business has written and designed. But it is more rewarding and probably more effective for the business if you discuss publicity with your clients, find out what they want to say and you yourself extract an interesting news point to put in a press or news release.

You then become more than simply a glorified typist. You need to be able to recognise an interesting piece of news and to write it up into an interesting press release. Or be able to suggest an event to which the media might want to send reporters or photographers. Or suggest when a letter might be sent to the press.

Writing copy for brochures, leaflets and sales letters does require special skills. Freelance copywriter Christine Hodgeson says:

> People say it's easy to write advertising copy. But if you look at what people who don't know much about it produce, they break every rule in the book.
>
> There is a certain amount of theory. There is also formula writing to a degree because there are certain rules you have to follow.
>
> I feel you should go on a couple of courses or have had some in-house training.

If you think that you can make a good fist of your own publicity, why not offer to do other people's? (There is more information about publicising your own business in Chapter 14.)

WHAT EQUIPMENT DO YOU NEED?

The beauty of this kind of work is that you only need your computer, printer and a word processing program. If your program includes templates or style sheets of the kind described in Chapter 3 which would help you design a basic news release, so much the better. A design package can help you to produce a nice-looking leaflet. But all this can be done with a simple word processing package. Mary Spencer, a freelance press agent, uses basic equipment:

> I use a 386 IBM-compatible computer and an ink jet printer. I find that my word processing program copes with virtually all the material I need to produce. Usually my clients supply their own business headed paper. But when they don't, I produce correctly headed paper using the templates supplied with my word processing program.
>
> Occasionally I design leaflets or small posters. Although my software does include a basic drawing package it is not very sophisticated. I am thinking of getting a proper DTP program. They do seem to be rather complicated so I may need to get some training in it.

Christine Hodgeson says firmly, 'I couldn't do my job without my PC!'

Below is a summary of what you can offer your clients.

NEWS RELEASE (PRESS RELEASE)

The basic part of any publicity campaign is the press release. This consists of one or two sheets of information about your clients and their services which you hope will be of interest to the media. It should contain a major piece of information which will inform, interest or entertain – preferably all three.

Getting the ideas

You need to discuss with your client what aspects of the business they are keen to publicise. Is it just general publicity that is required or is there one aspect which your client is keen to play up? Is the publicity required long term (encourage that for regular work!), or just for one particular event or period of time?

Then you need to discuss the nature of the business and decide what you are going to use in the publicity. If there is a particular event coming up then that is more straightforward than thinking of new things to say month after month.

Make sure you fully understand your client's needs and what the business does. Make a note of any names and dates needed – nothing annoys clients more than seeing their name spelt wrongly so make sure that it won't be *your* fault.

Ask for any literature produced by the business that will help you. Mary Spencer says:

I always take some time to discuss with my clients what exactly they want from their publicity so that I can tailor it precisely to their needs.

I usually deal with the client's publicity contact with the press. So I need to get to know enough about each client's business to enable me to answer questions about it. I liaise with my clients when arranging photo opportunities or interviews.

Pick out one aspect to publicise in each news release, for example perhaps your client has just won an award for their service or goods. Use one major point only. If you try to put in two or more points you will confuse people and the publicity is less likely to be of use.

News release format

The common term for a news release used to be 'press release'. But as that seems to excludes radio and TV it is usual now to use the word 'news'.

A news release is easy to produce and there is a set formula. Head an A4 sheet of paper clearly 'News release' because that tells the editors of papers or TV and radio producers that your client does not expect payment. Make sure that your client's name, address, phone and fax numbers are on the top of the page, together with the business name if that is different. If you are to be answering any phone calls from the media then you should add your name and phone number as a 'contact'. If your client has business paper it is better to use that if possible and to add the words 'NEWS RELEASE' in capitals under the business heading.

Then put the date. This is so that editors can decide how relevant the news is. You can write a release three times if the event is newsworthy enough – it will happen, it is just about to happen, it has happened – but if you have a release dated three months before or after an event, that is hardly likely to be news!

Put a title to the release. This will probably not be used, but will give an idea of the content of your release. Make sure that the body of your release is double-spaced with 2.5 cm margins so that it is easy to read. Try to keep it to one side of an A4 sheet, but if you need to carry on put 'more follows' or 'mf' at the foot of the page. Centred under the last line write 'END' and below that, next to the margin, repeat your name and phone number.

Make sure each sheet is numbered and contains a word from the heading, e.g. 'writer-2'.

The content of the release should contain the five Ws of journalism – Who, What, Where, When and Why. If there is space, or it is particularly relevant or interesting, you can add the 'How' last of all. All the necessary information should be contained in the first paragraph. The other paragraphs elaborate on the first and it should be possible to cut them without losing the story.

So a basic release for one client might read:

Direct mail expert, John Jackson [the who] won an industry merit award [the what] on Thursday 9 November [the when]. Mr Jackson received his prize at Micklesham town hall [the where] where it was given in recognition of his innovative improvements to the direct mail business [the why]. Mr Jackson improved the speed of direct mail businesses by introducing the through-flow-backstop system which increases the speed of direct mail production by 35 per cent [the how].

You can add a background information sheet about your client's business if you think editors would find it helpful.

Use your computer to print out as many copies as you need to send to the local press, radio and TV, as well as magazines specialising in your client's business. Try to angle the releases to each type of media. For example for local media emphasise the local aspect 'Local Micklesham man invents. . .' and for the specialist media play on your client's expertise in the subject 'database expert Sally . . .'.

Look in the *Writers' and Artists' Yearbook* (A & C Black) or the *Writer's Handbook* (Macmillan) for details of magazines. Use *British Rate and Data (BRAD)* or *Willings Press Guide* for information about local media. All these should be available in your public library. Address your letters to the editor by name if possible, otherwise to 'the editor'.

If your client wants to handle any press interest then you need do no more. But if you are in charge of a client's publicity you will need to keep a copy of the release by your phone so that if a reporter calls you to check facts or arrange an interview with your client you have the information in front of you. Make a list of any useful information a reporter might want to know.

Don't include photos with a press release unless they are exceptionally good. If you do they should be black and white, 10 in x 8 in, glossy, and with a caption stuck (not written) on the back. Avoid getting your fingerprints on the photo! In practice if a paper is interested in having a photo of your client they will send their own photographer.

Send the releases to:

- national radio, TV, press – try to target the editors of particular sections such as education editor or business editor, or the producer or organiser of particular programs;
- local press, radio and TV;
- relevant trade papers;
- relevant consumer magazines;
- relevant hobby magazines;
- business magazines.

Addresses for all these can be found in *The Writers' and Artists' Yearbook*, *The Writer's Handbook*, *BRAD* or *Willings*.

Unless you have good media contacts, or your client has a particularly newsworthy or visually exciting piece of news, you are unlikely to get national publicity. In that case concentrate on the other sources in the list above.

☐ **Suggest to your clients that they should not be too proud to send information to small publications such as church magazines, club newsletters, freesheets (also listed in *BRAD* and *Willings*) etc. Nobody can afford to ignore good local publicity.**

LEAFLETS

Your client may want you to write up and produce leaflets advertising the business, or to send to potential or regular clients. Or you may be asked to produce a certain number of leaflets based on material your client has designed. In this case you can produce the leaflet on your PC but arrange to have large numbers printed at your local printers (and charged to your client).

Leaflets can be one or two sided and in black and white or colour. They can also be A4 sheets folded in half or thirds. Obviously one side in black and white is going to be cheaper. Illustrations will be cheaper if they are line drawings in black and white rather than in colour or photos.

> ☐ **Use style sheets or templates for producing leaflets.**

If you have a sophisticated computer and printer then you can produce quite complicated colour leaflets but these will usually be cheaper to produce by a printer if you need more than a dozen. Any computer can produce a simple one-sided black and white leaflet, although again for speed and lower cost ask your printer first.

Make sure that your client's business name is near the top and clear, and that you have included a contact name together with address, phone number and fax number. The name and address of the publisher (your client) and printer must, by law, appear in small print at the bottom (see page 151).

Content of leaflet

What is the main point of a leaflet? Is your client offering a service? You may want a large heading 'Cut-price database service'. Or is your client selling something? Then try 'Buy xxx – special offer'. Follow with a brief explanation of the service or product your client is offering. Keep the lettering clear and reasonably large. You need to catch people's eyes. Then tell the customers how they can use your client's service or obtain the product. Should they phone you or fill in a form at the bottom of the leaflet?

Design your leaflet in rough before you try it on the screen. When you are satisfied with it either run off copies or take it to a printer to use as a master copy.

☐ **Many word processing packages now enable you to print copy in a large number of different typefaces or fonts. Do not use more than two different typefaces or your leaflet will look messy. You can achieve a clear and sophisticated effect with just one typeface in different sizes, and using bold, italic or capitals.**

SALES LETTERS

These are persuasive letters usually sent to mailing list customers or potential customers. How much writing you do will depend on your customers. Copywriter Christine Hodgeson says:

Some people know what they want and others don't.

Some people give me a pretty tight brief – marketing companies, for instance, know what they want and have fairly fixed ideas.

Small businesses, on the other hand, may be happy to leave the copywriting to you.

Use your client's business headed notepaper which should be clear and not gimmicky. Try to address someone in the firm or household by name. Ask a question in the first paragraph 'Do you need extra help with your accounts?' and tell the customer who your client is and what they do: 'I am a freelance accountant who can offer an overnight auditing service to local businesses.' Give details of your client's prices: 'My rates are competitive at £xxx for this service' and say how he or she is better than anyone else in your field: 'This service is unique in the Barchester area.' Make sure what you claim is true – remember the Trades Description Act.

Advertising experts tell us that the PS at the end of a sales letter is the most often read and remembered part, so always add one: 'PS For the next three months I can offer my services for only £xxx'.

POSTERS

You can use your PC to produce small A4 posters. Any smaller and they cannot be seen in a window; any larger and your PC printer is unlikely to be able to cope with them. Your client may want them for handing out to shops to put in their windows or for local organisations to pin up in their meeting places.

If you are asked to produce complicated, multi-coloured designs you should only accept this kind of work if you have a laser colour printer and good design experience. As copy like this will need to be printed commercially from your design you will need to understand and be able to produce colour separations, that is different parts of the design in one of the four colours used in printing – cyan, black, magenta and yellow – which are then combined in the printing process to produce the final, full-coloured result.

If you have doubt about your ability to do this then only offer black and white work. You can then either produce the copies yourself if your printer is of high enough quality or else take it to a commercial printer for printing in large numbers. Mary Spencer says:

> Most of my work is involved with producing press releases because that is the area in which small businesses do not have much experience. It is surprising how much publicity can be obtained for even a very small business.
>
> Although I do have media contacts which helps, it is possible for someone without them to do publicity work. You just have to work harder at getting to know people and getting a reputation as a reliable source of information. Being confident on the phone helps, of course. It's no good being shy about talking to reporters or following up a press release.

WHERE TO FIND WORK

Your obvious outlets are small local businesses or self-employed people who do not have the money or facilities to deal with their own publicity. You could also advertise your services to such people as authors, artists and crafts people countrywide through their specialist magazines. Clubs and organisations may need your services, as might schools and colleges on particular occasions. Your services may be used long term or on one-off occasions.

EARNINGS

The amount you can earn depends on you. Large organisations are prepared to pay large sums of money for PR work. Smaller businesses will not have that kind of spare money.

You could charge by the day or by the project. It is probably safer to charge by the day because you may not be able to gauge accurately how long you will need to work on a particular piece of publicity. Mary Spencer advises:

> I used to charge per project when I started but now I charge per day. I would advise people just starting to work out what you want to earn per hour and then cost that over half a day.

You could charge per item for writing and printing so many copies of leaflets or posters, or for preparing, printing and sending letters. Ask around to find out what other people charge and charge a bit less to get started then increase your rate as you get more experience. Don't price yourself out of the market.

11

READY-
PROGRAMMED
SOFTWARE

So FAR THIS BOOK has told you how to make money with your computer by using the main groups of software – word processing programs, spreadsheets, databases, mail merge and DTP programs.

But you can also buy ready-made packages that will set you up with your own business from the start. Each self-contained product includes software dedicated to a particular business activity and full instructions about how to use it. With your computer and software supplied by these firms you can create your own business.

Many people have spent considerable time thinking up new marketing ploys for PC users. For example, how would you like to run a travel agency, make wills, predict the future, draw up a family tree or compile crosswords using your PC at home? All these and many more ideas are possible.

Sometimes the work involves producing documents such as astrological charts or wills to a customer's details, or creating a database for matching customers with goods or services, or using programs where your computer connects to a central database which you access to answer telephone enquiries.

WHERE TO FIND IDEAS

Many home business magazines such as *Home Business* or *Home Run* publish articles on people who make money using their PCs. *Home Business* in particular is a source of ads for PC users. PC magazines also contain ads offering 'work from home' software. Just reading through the advertisements will give you an idea of the range of things you can do. The classified ads of the national papers are also worth looking at, particularly for the larger franchised operations such as a home-based travel agency.

Here are a few examples of selling points from real advertisements and articles.

... a straightforward business opportunity that requires any IBM-compatible computer and printer, a TOTAL investment of £25 and a few hours of your time ...

... a personalised book business of your own. After the story is printed using a computer and laser printer, the books are bound. ... The start-up package is £1,495.00.

The package comprises special software which works out the configuration of the planets and stars at the moment of a client's birth, from which a page of information can be printed ...

Turn your computer into gold! With a package of 12 different horoscopes ...

Do you own an IBM-compatible computer and

printer? If you do then it could earn you a substantial income in a very short span . . . your once-only investment is £30. . . . This includes all the software and manuals that you will need.

We are an established firm of independent and bonded flight and travel agents. . . . You need to own an IBM-compatible personal computer to access our centrally maintained databases. Your total financial involvement is limited to . . . £1,350.00 . . .

The perfect CV computer kit £36.95 . . .

Will writing by computer. Earns up to £75 an hour.

All these are genuine offers. In fact, practically any home-based computer job you can think of has already had software written for it and is being offered to an eager audience.

Danger Points

Many of these offers are made in good faith and with work on your part will live up to their claims. But you do need to be aware of certain problems and dangers.

Multi-level marketing (MLM)

If you are thinking about following up offers from magazines, one area you need to be careful about is multi-level marketing. A number of ads for PC operated businesses work in this way. MLM is also known as network selling. It has had an extremely bad reputation, which the industry has been taking steps to improve.

MLM works on the network marketing principle. One person sells the product and also sells the product distribution rights to several other people. Those people in turn sell the product and sell on the distribution rights to several more people, and so on, thus expanding the selling base. The selling of the actual product can become incidental to the creation of the sales force.

These schemes rely heavily on people continuing to sell on the distribution rights. It only takes a few people to 'break the chain' for it to fail to work as advertised. In that case the people who start the network make money, while those further along may make very little and get left with a lot of unsaleable stock.

Some small ads which claim that their project is not MLM are in fact misleading. They often turn out to be network marketing in another form only this time selling software which in turn produces leaflets about the system. The software is sold on or 'registered' with the first person and then the next people on the list sell their software/brochure on. One scheme I investigated operated on exactly this system.

These smaller schemes sometimes eliminate any product as such and ask you to pay a 'registration fee' to add your name to a list as a 'vendor'. Like a chain letter your name goes on the bottom and moves up as new people enter the chain. Each new person who joins is expected to send money to the other people on this list. Your name stays on until it reaches the top.

Serious MLM or network selling enterprises have no fear about telling people about the nature of their scheme. They have to operate under the strict regulations of the Fair Trading Act 1973. Beware of those which don't admit to being MLM schemes and turn out to be so or those which state, 'This is *not* network selling' without telling you what it *is*. (To check on a company, contact the Office of Fair

Trading or the Direct Selling Association, listed under Useful Addresses.)

Some sellers claim that because users have to register with them the law is not being broken. Even so, the system is fallible and preys on the gullibility of not very bright and often not very well off people.

My advice is, don't touch chain letter MLM schemes. They are unlikely to bring you the amount of money claimed and are morally suspect.

Hard work is needed

Many of the other schemes in the ads will work, but a lot will depend on how much effort you put into it. Like any job that you want to earn a lot of money from you have to put in plenty of hard work yourself. You will not get rich simply by sending off for the package and turning out a few examples.

You will need to spend a lot of time learning how to use the product and making sure that you can package it pleasantly. You will need to put a lot of work in to publicising your product and demonstrating it. When you do get work you must be quick, reliable and reasonably priced.

Costs

Every home computer job will have some minimal start-up costs. Assuming you have the basic PC/printer set-up, every job needs extras. For example, for word processing work you will need to buy paper, envelopes, folders, stamps and labels. For telesales, which involves transmitting clients' orders to a central company computer, you will need a modem. And so on.

The ads assume that you have the basic PC set-up but they also ask you to pay a set-up fee which allows you to buy the necessary software for the scheme they are selling. This, as you can see from the examples above, can range from a small sum to a thousand pounds or more. But assuming that you buy a reasonably priced package, your start up costs should be small.

Before you buy one of these packages you should make sure that you really want to do it and that you can afford the package. Check the product out – ask for a demonstration. Ask for references from other clients whom you should contact for an honest opinion and information about the pitfalls. Find out whether the package will mean you need to buy expensive extra hardware such as a modem before you can use it.

You may decide that the price involved is small enough for you to take the risk. But for those packages demanding large set-up fees it is wise to be cautious.

Inadequate instructions or guarantees

Whereas the branded commercial software comes with hefty and full instructions, and guarantees for replacement if the product does not work, this may not be the case with software from small companies or personal ads.

The instructions may be limited to a couple of typed sheets and if the disk is faulty or the program refuses to do what it claims it may be difficult, if not impossible, to reclaim either your money or a replacement disk, whatever the law says.

☐ **Before you spend any money on software that is not from one of the large commercial companies make sure that you thoroughly check what is being offered, and what guarantees and instructions the supplier will include.**

Beware of false claims

You can often spot a dubious ad by the fact that it does not tell you what the business concept is. It will simply say something like 'Earn thousands of pounds with your computer. We supply the software, you make the money. Guaranteed winner.' It will not mention any product or service and will not tell you how the money is to be made. Be careful of ads like these. If the concept was not in any way dubious the advertiser would be quite happy to tell you what the business would involve.

FRANCHISES

Some of the ready-made opportunities for PC users, such as a home-based travel agency, use the franchise system of starting a business. You should be aware of the advantages and disadvantages of this system.

What is a franchise?

A franchise is usually a business format franchise. This is a package that includes the entire business concept, including the use of a common name or shop sign and the uniform presentation of contract premises and/or means of transport, training and continued help. It is designed so that someone who is untrained in the business can be helped to set up and run the business. The franchisee will invest in the business and own it, but will continue to pay the franchiser for continuing rights to use the concept.

The person who owns the rights to the franchise concept is called the franchiser. They decide how the business should be run, how and what goods or services will be offered, what standards of performance are required, the price structure, the design of any premises and stationery, and any other ways the business is presented to the public. Macdonalds and Body Shop are examples of successful major companies who offer franchises. They operate strict guidelines on how the franchise must be run and provide an immediately recognisable corporate identity.

You can buy this formula for successfully running the business. You then become the franchisee. You pay a set-up fee and a royalty to the franchiser, but in return you usually receive help in setting up the business and continued help after that.

A more common use of the word franchise nowadays includes any transaction in which one person licenses another person with the rights to do something. It may not include all the help given in a business format franchise.

When deciding whether to take on a franchise make sure you find out exactly what kind of franchise is being offered. A business format franchise may cost more in the long run, but may be more reliable.

There are usually two stages to acquiring a franchise. First you pay for the services you need before you can start the business. This should include the necessary training. Then you should have a continuing relationship with the franchise owner who should offer help and advice.

The advantages of buying a franchise are that most of the potential problems should have been sorted out and the risks eliminated as far as possible. Also information about how to run the business is set out in detail for you.

The disadvantages are that you may be deserted after paying for the initial stage. This is more common with the general licensing franchise. If you are asked for a great deal of money for the first stage you should be wary. Make sure that you get any contract checked by a solicitor and that there are safeguards against unfulfilled promises. If possible, talk to other franchise holders in the same company.

TYPICAL SOFTWARE PACKAGES

There are a number of software money-making packages regularly offered in PC and home business magazines. Although in practice there are an endless variety of home business packages suitable for PC users, the following seem to be perennially popular.

CVs

CVs have been mentioned in more detail in Chapter 3. You don't actually need special software to produce well-designed CVs, although obviously if you can work with a specially designed template or style sheet this will make your job quicker and easier. Setting out presentable and clear CVs is an art in itself. A CV package will provide you with one or more layouts for CVs with guidance on how to fill one in for each client. The suitably printed result is designed to impress potential employers.

Family trees

This software allows you to generate and print family trees either in 'book' form (that is the tree is written down in words rather than as a diagram) or in the form of the usual family tree diagrams. You can also get software to generate circular trees.

You need to spend a lot of time keying in data either from raw lists given to you by your client or by culling the information from a hand-drawn tree.

It helps if you have some understanding of genealogy so that you can pick up obvious mistakes. If you are going to offer more than simply keying in dates, which the software will translate into a tree for you, then you will need to take an accredited course in genealogy and become a qualified genealogist. If you do this then you can research into the client's family and then use that data to produce a final tree. You would charge for research time as well as generating the end product. But it is possible to provide the end product simply as a nicely printed tree from the client's data.

Heraldry

There are now packages offered in some PC magazines that will enable you to produce coats of arms. As a Windows-based package heraldry software provides all the symbols, shapes and colours necessary for you to produce a coat of arms. You do need a PC with a Windows environment, as well as a hard disk and VGA monitor.

☐ **Heraldry has many technical terms. Read a book on the subject to help you understand what you are doing.**

You can earn money with this program as an extra option with a genealogy program or as a service on its own. Many people are interested in their family name and would like to buy a picture of the coat of arms associated with that name. It would be best with a colour printer to get the full effect of the colourful nature of the designs. You can offer to provide coats of arms for any family name and then look up the description in any standard book of arms. Some of the more detailed books have descriptions but no illustrations which is why knowing the correct heraldic term for each heraldic symbol and colour is important. You can also produce the design from descriptions sent to you by your customers.

Fortune telling

Under this heading come a variety of fun business opportunities. You could produce astrological birth charts, provide a printed sheet telling someone's future, give a palm reading or tell the tarot cards. All these, and variations on them, are supplied as complete software packages both for business use and fun.

With an astrological chart package, for example, you are provided with software that guides you step by step through all the information to be put into the program for each client, such as date, time and place of birth. The program would then do the calculations and at the end you can print out a nice-looking chart.

If this is something you would enjoy as a way of using your PC for making money then you will need a good choice of products. You would not have to meet clients as they could supply you with all the information by post or over the phone.

Compiling crosswords

Crossword compilers can and do use computers not only for writing the clues but also for generating the grids and it is possible to buy special software for the purpose. You can either present your crosswords complete with the grid by using such programs or simply send in the clues and solutions if the paper or magazine provides its own grids.

Of course, you do need to be able to compile crosswords! The only way to learn this is to do it. There are books on the subject but you need to be able to understand clues.

☐ **Solve as many crosswords as you can before you try to compile your own.**

Pat Duncan, a professional crossword compiler, says:

> I started compiling crosswords when I was still at
> school. My first paid crossword was when I was 15.
>
> I use my word processing program to do the clues
> and the solutions on my computer. I send clients a
> page of clues and a page of solutions. One of the good
> things is that if I'm syndicating work I can send out
> top copies, as it were, to all of a dozen clients.
>
> People can do grids on the computer but I haven't
> found it necessary to do so. That works at the other
> end. The newspaper can produce the grids on *its*
> computer.
>
> My business has undoubtedly improved since I
> started using a computer. It's made me much more
> productive. It enables me to produce much more work
> in terms of sales to clients.
>
> Clients treat me as a serious operator because it
> looks more professional – it *is* more professional.

Will writing

A typical will writing software package will provide you with
legally valid documents and a library of clauses, as well as a
tutorial on how to use the package and advice on advertising.
Many people want to make wills without going to solicitors or
paying high fees so this could be a good way to earn money.
But you must read the tutorial carefully because if you
produce a legally invalid will for your client or one that does
not say what is wanted you will cause a lot of anguish. You
may also find yourself financially liable for any mistakes you
make unless you give careful disclaimers. Look into the
possibility of insuring against mistakes.

Pools forecasts

There are people who will pay you to forecast football results so that they can fill in their pools coupons. You can buy ready-made software packages to do just that. If you do offer this service you must make clear that you cannot guarantee the results. But if you are astray too often you will lose your customers.

> ☐ **Try out any such package on your own behalf first of all. When you are satisfied that you and it together are achieving a reasonable result regularly enough to offer to the public then you can set up in business. This is a form of gambling with all the uncertainties that entails, but in spite of that many of your customers will expect you to be right more often than not.**

Travel agency

One of the many larger scale business opportunities for PC users is running a home-based travel agency. You can do this via a franchise. This can be a good way of getting into the business because the franchise owner gives a lot of help and support.

Typically your job would be to offer clients appropriate and competitive airline fares worldwide. Your computer connects to the franchise owner's central computer where you have access to its databases. You should expect to get a training seminar, computer/database seminar, an initial supply of the firm's stationery including necessary enquiry and receipt forms, all necessary brochures and guides, dedicated computer software and a suppliers' list. You would be expected to attract your own customers.

You will need at least a 286 PC, a phone and a modem. As you get more customers you will probably need to add a fax and an answering machine.

Personalised books

Some ads offer you the chance to create personalised books, that is, books with the customer's name inserted in place of that of the hero or heroine, together with details of their house, pets, friends etc.

For example, a sentence might read 'One day [client's name] walked along [client's street] and met [client's friends].'

You get the necessary software and, in some more expensive deals, the PC and printer too. With the help of the seller you create a paperback or hardback book to the customer's order. You do need to find out whether binding is included in the deal or whether you have to pay the firm extra for this service.

These types of books are very popular as gifts for children and adult versions are also available.

OTHER BRIGHT IDEAS

If you do not want to run an already established business and none of the other ideas in this book appeals to you, look at your own interests and hobbies, and see if you can adapt them to computer work. Or look at other ideas in home business magazines and see if you can use a computer to make them work.

> ☐ **There may already be software to help you even if it has not been written with a business in mind. Whatever hobby or interest you have, someone somewhere has probably designed software to help you. Shareware disks, advertised in PC magazines, are a particularly good source of help.**

Look at these ideas which all use a home PC for running the business:

- running a lost key service. Clients' keys are identified by individual numbers. Details of these together with the owners' names and addresses are kept in a PC database so that lost keys sent to you can be returned to their owners.

- a book-finding service. Lists of customers and their book requests are kept on a PC and matched with suppliers' lists as well as used as a basis for your own book searches. When the relevant volumes have been located, customers are offered the chance to buy them.

- running a pen-pal service. Lists of people looking for pen-pals are kept in a PC database and individuals are matched according to their interests and requests and put in touch with each other.

- selling racing forecasts. Racing forecasts worked out by means of a PC program are sold to customers.

- translation work. This involves translation to or from a foreign language, either from your own knowledge or with the help of a PC language translation program. If you have a modem or fax, work can be transmitted directly to clients.

- property letting. A list of properties to let is kept on a PC and matched with customers' property needs.

- invoice service. This involves sending out printed invoices for clients. Many word processing programs provide invoice templates.

- copy-editing. Preparing text for a printer or publisher.

- indexing. Creating indexes for books, reports, etc. There are indexing programs available for PCs.

EARNINGS

Your income will depend on what type of computer job package you buy and how much work you put into the job. In theory you can make unlimited amounts from MLM! As far as crosswords go, this varies from paper to paper.

12

SELLING COMPUTER EXPERTISE

So FAR I have talked about how you can make money with the programs you have on your computer. But it is possible to make money by using the computer itself.

You may be one of those people who have had a PC for a few years and have spent a lot of time experimenting with it. You may well have learnt a lot that you can offer other people.

PC engineers have to go through training before they mess about with the insides of other people's computers. Some companies such as Lotus do offer courses in computer maintenance but these can be expensive. Unless you are a trained PC engineer I do not advise you to offer this kind of work! However, if you know or have learnt a lot about how to set up a PC for use, and about using the various kinds of software on offer, then you can sell this advice to others.

PC TROUBLE-SHOOTER

You may think you know about PCs and be able to offer good advice. How can you tell whether you are good enough? Answer these questions.

- Can you set up any PC and get it ready to work?
- Can you get practically any PC software to work?
- Are you good at solving software problems?
- Do you keep up to date with PCs and software use?
- Do other people ask you for advice?
- Do you enjoy meeting people?

If you can answer 'yes' to all these questions then you should be able to cope with consultancy.

What is computer consultancy?

In this context computer consultancy is making yourself and your expertise available to others, either in your own home or in your customers' homes. You can give advice about how to set up PCs, how to load and use software, how to get the best out of software or how to solve problems that stop software working properly. Many people would be glad of your help and be willing to pay for the advice.

You do not need to have special training, although obviously if you have been to PC classes of any kind this would help. Michael Cattell, PC trouble-shooter, is self-taught and says:

> I'd been tinkering around with computers for a few years, and friends and colleagues of mine who've got computers kept asking me to help them out. In the

end, with one of my colleagues, I decided I could make a little business of it. I just do it in the evenings.

Michael Cattell does not offer services to businesses but to local PC users:

The service I offer is to people who've bought a computer, have got it home full of enthusiasm and don't know what to do with it. Or what they want to do with it doesn't happen. With a lot of software, especially games software which is memory hungry, it's very difficult to configure the computer to work it. So I offer a service of actually going round to their homes and sorting their problems out.

What equipment do you need?

The only equipment you will need is your own PC and software if you are demonstrating at home, or your customer's PC and software if you are visiting their homes. If you go to their homes your job is to use their equipment so that they can see what to do with it. In your home you should ask them to bring along their software so that you can demonstrate how to use it on your machine.

What skills do you need?

The skills you need are those which were pinpointed in the questions above. You need to be well versed in how PCs work and how to get software to work on them. You need to be able to solve problems with software, and explain to people how to get the best out of it and their PC. You need to be able to explain all this to complete beginners in a way that they will understand, without talking down to them. Most of all you need to be able to get on well with people.

Where to find work

There are people all over the UK who are exasperated by their inability to use their PC and software as they would wish. You can, like Michael Cattell, confine yourself to local work or advertise more widely. Local papers are a good start and may provide you enough work on its own. Or you could advertise in regional papers in areas to which you can travel easily.

You will have to meet customers, either in your home or theirs, so don't cast your net too widely, otherwise you will find travelling too time-consuming and cost-inefficient.

How much can you earn?

You should charge by the hour for this service. You may want to charge more if you have to do a lot of travelling or a bit less if your customers come to you.

SELLING PROGRAMS

You may, like my son, enjoy writing programs for your PC. Programs involve writing the set of software instructions to the PC which will tell it to perform a certain task. This task could be useful, such as a simplified form of bookkeeping, or a game. Many people start by compiling programs in a straightforward computer language such as Basic. But if you are hoping to sell your programs commercially you will need to learn to use one of the faster, number-based machine code programs. You may invent your own games or useful programs (called 'utilities' in PC magazines). If you do and you think they are good enough for other people to use then you could consider selling them.

The more specialised you can make your programs for utilities the better. For example, a program to solve a specific problem encountered by people trying to keep a record of their cows' milk yield may sell better than yet another bookkeeping program.

Of course, any software you sell as your own must be your original work and not copied from any other program otherwise you might get sued.

What equipment do you need?

You need your PC and software which enables you to use a machine code programming language. If you are intending to sell games then you will probably need a colour VDU because most people expect games to be in colour nowadays. If you are providing a utility, perhaps a simple program to produce crossword grids, then you can use mono.

As you hope to sell these programs you will need disks to copy the programs on to and labels for the disks giving your name and copyright notice and address, as well as information about the contents. You should get these specially printed or run them off on your printer so that they look professional and inspire confidence in their contents.

You will also need special plastic sleeves to protect the disks and cardboard disk envelopes to protect them in transit.

As well as the disk you should write a guide to using the program and print it out for each customer.

What skills do you need?

You need to have a logical mind and to understand how to use a computer programming language. This is something you can teach yourself from books, although you may find it helpful to take a course in programming. There are also software programs that will help you program in easy stages.

You need to be methodical because each command follows

on from the rest. If you miss one out or write it wrongly, the program won't work!

For programming utilities you need to have a clear idea of what you want to achieve and the steps the program will need to go through. If you want to invent games you need to be imaginative and be able to produce pictures, the more complicated the better.

Where to sell your programs

You can try sending your programs to commercial companies who advertise in PC magazines, but don't expect much joy. Although people have made a fortune like this it is rare. Large companies employ people to program utilities and games for them. It is better to market them yourself. Then if it is a success, you reap all the profit!

A better bet is to advertise your own programs in PC magazines or in magazines related to your program. So, if you invent a new way of drawing up a horoscope, for example, you could advertise in both home business magazines and astrology magazines. You could also offer your programs to shareware companies.

Earnings

You can sell your programs as shareware through ads in magazines. You then charge a few pounds to buy the disk and a basic instruction leaflet, and ask customers to send you a higher fee to register as a user. You then send them the full instructions and information about any updates you make in the future.

The snag about shareware is that the customer may not send you the extra money. You have no way of knowing whether they really didn't like the program or simply don't want to pay more.

You can also just set a price on your program and advertise

it as such. You then need to pay for the cost of the advertisement, but may recoup more in the long run. You then send the customer the disk and full instructions in one go.

Don't forget to take into account the cost of the packaging and postage when setting the price for your disks.

If you do manage to sell a program to a major software company then the sky's your limit!

FILE AND DISK CONVERSION

Many of the more powerful word processing programs include the ability to change files from one computer language to another. This is a service that you can offer once you feel confident about using your particular program. If your present program doesn't offer this facility it is possible to buy software that converts to and from virtually all the most used languages, including the universal language ASCII.

Disk formatting

You can take this further by converting PC formatted disks and files for Mac and PCW use, and vice versa. Again software is available for this.

Because disks come in several sizes you can offer to transfer information from say 5.25 inch disks to 3.5 inch disks or the other way. But for this you will need a disk drive (slot into which you put your floppy disk) for both sizes. Most PCs will have a spare slot for an extra drive which your dealer can fit for you. Or you can buy external disk drives in both sizes that attach to the outside of your PC by a cable.

Scanning images

If you have a powerful scanner you can offer to scan images on to disks for other people who do not have their own or whose scanner does not give a good enough image. They can then insert the scanned image into their own program.

Skills you need

You need to be competent in the use of file conversion and disk formatting software. This is usually straightforward and is explained in your owner's manual. You need to be able to copy disks. This, too, is usually part of your computer's operating system.

Where to find work

PC magazines often advertise these kinds of services. They are good places to sell your skills. Many people have PCs or PCWs on which they cannot use certain disks or programs. By offering to convert their disks and programs you are providing a valuable service. Not everybody has the latest software and PC. Also, many people who have upgraded their PC, or changed for example from PC to Mac or vice versa, will have disks they cannot use and work they cannot read.

Earnings

If you are offering to convert files or disks or scan on to a disk charge a fee per disk.

13

TELEWORKING TECHNIQUES

IT IS POSSIBLE to use your PC to continue your full-time job at home. If your employer is amenable to this idea they may agree to you continuing to do the same work as before, but from your home and using your own PC. Many people are beginning to work in this way and companies are beginning to appreciate the advantages of having a happy, home-based work force. You will need your PC, a telephone, and perhaps a fax and answering machine. The company may pay for these. BT is a pioneer of this kind of PC work and most of its directory enquiry operators now work from home.

TELEWORKERS

There is a new breed of homeworkers, called teleworkers, who depend on their phone and their computer to continue their jobs and to keep themselves in touch with the world. The term also includes self-employed PC users who keep in touch with their clients in this way.

Teleworkers are catered for by their own Telecottage

Association and its magazine, *Teleworker*, (see 'Useful addresses', below). The Telecottage Association defines teleworking as 'working at a distance from your employer, either at home, or at a locally based centre. Teleworkers use computers, telephones and faxes to keep in contact with their employers and customers.' So you, as someone working at home making money from your PC, are a teleworker. In the USA this is called telecommuting.

Teleworking does not have to mean that you necessarily have to go 'on-line', that is when the computer and/or fax is connected by a modem to the phone so that they can talk directly to other computers. But being 'on-line' has many advantages such as speed of communication, and access to other computers and data. This is now something that you as a teleworker might want to consider.

WHAT KIND OF WORK CAN YOU DO?

There are many kinds of work you can do in this way, apart from freelance PC work. The range of work that can be done by teleworkers is very wide. A common use is for sales people. They can access the company main computer for information about stock and orders. You often see this now in shops where an assistant will call up stock on a computer and record the sale immediately with an instant alteration to the stock holding.

Similar uses can be seen in sales of tickets for theatres, holiday reservations or travel companies who check plane seat availability before issuing tickets.

In fact any job that requires access to large amounts of

information either for sale or simply for relaying to others is ideal for teleworking.

But many other jobs can be done in the same way. Accounts can be done at home and sent to the employer via the telephone. Designers can send their plans from the computer to their employer or client directly down the phone.

Another use of the telephone for a homeworker with a computer is computer conferencing. This enables a number of computers to be connected via the telephone. By typing on to your screen the writing appears on all other screens so that a number of computer users can 'talk' to each other. This has been tried successfully with distance learning, for example, where a teacher can hold a seminar with a number of students, all of whom study from home. A few other examples are listed below:

- credit and stock control;
- auditing;
- systems support and development;
- engineering and technical design;
- real-time inventory;
- sales analysis;
- school inspection reports;
- council correspondence;
- specialist managerment.

HOW DO YOU START?

If you still go out to work, one way to start in this field is to find out whether your employer can arrange this kind of work for you. In that case you will get help in setting up the right kind of system compatible with your work and will get the necessary software. The cost to your employer for setting you up with dedicated software, and for providing a phone, business line, fax and answering machine would not be great.

☐ **If you are going to work for yourself then you should include in your calculations the setting up costs in addition to any extra equipment you may need for your computer.**

ISDN

The system can be speeded up by using the new ISDN (integrated services digital network) system. These are new kinds of lines which can transmit more data at higher speeds. They are more expensive to install and rent, but they can support the use of several machines at once. So you can run a fax, computer and phone off one of these lines instead of having to use them one at a time. Imogen Bertin, a teleworker writer and designer, likes ISDN:

> The advantage of ISDN is that you can have one ISDN line and hang a whole series of devices off it. This includes a group 4 fax which is something that is extremely useful for teleworkers who are working in the publishing area. Those are much better quality than ordinary faxes. So, on your ISDN line you could, for example, have a group 4 fax, your computer, telephone and answerphone. Although it's more expensive you can have these devices all talking at once.

Not all organisations provide work in this way. But if you think that your work could just as easily be done at home by means of a computer and phone link then you could discuss this with your employer.

GOING ON-LINE

For many teleworkers the best way of working is to go on-line. This means that you can have direct access to other PCs via your PC and a modem to connect you to a phone line. But get advice about setting up your modem or you may waste its potential. They are tricky to connect correctly to your PC. They can also be time-wasting if you discover that you enjoy using them to 'talk' to fellow PC users! Imogen Bertin says:

> Lots of people have modems, but very few actually use them effectively. They're extremely difficult to set up. Once they're set up they're totally addictive and you start spending lots of money on on-line services, telephone bills and so on.

Your computer can be connected to a main computer, together with other people's so that you can access and input information. In this way you can have access to many other people's information. For example, you could get information from a central office computer without leaving home or read data from libraries all over the world. (Read Chapter 5 for more information about how to access databases on other computers.) Imogen Bertin is able to access databases for her work:

> The kind of work I do is a variety of writing and design services. For example, one of the things that I do is to prepare fax newsletters for a

telecommunications company. To do that I go on-line on the Dow Jones system in New York, extract news items and rewrite them. Then I print them out on a particular template because the thing has to look a particular way and be very clear because some people may get bad quality faxes. I print that out and I then fax that to a BT multi-fax in London, where it automatically gets re-sent to all the people on the subscription list.

For individuals who are self-employed using a modem can have its uses. You can connect to other people doing similar work, and exchange ideas and information. You can join with a partner on the other side of the country and work together using this system. Writers can write books together like this. Or you can use electronic mail to keep in touch with other computer users.

E-mail

Electronic mail or E-mail has been described in more detail in Chapter 5. By paying a fee you can join information groups that enable you to send messages to other users via your PC which they can read on their own computer screen. This can be very useful for obtaining information from a lot of people very quickly when they are a great distance away. These organisations also allow you to access, for example, library booklists or articles. You pay a yearly or monthly fee for joining and then pay according to the time you use the system. When using E-mail you have to pay for telephone connection time. If you also do on-line research, you will pay an hourly fee for searching the database and a fee for each record you download to your own computer. This can be quite expensive, but can still save time and money if the alternative is employing a researcher or making a long journey and doing the research yourself. If you can eventually afford a CD-ROM disk drive for your PC you will be able to read a great deal of information. CD-ROMs are compact disks with Read Only Memory. You can read information off them if you have a suitable disk drive, but you cannot store your own data on them. CDs can hold vast amounts of information (such as the entire contents of encyclopaedias) which can be useful for researchers. Systems will soon be available which will enable you to write to CDs and so store large amounts of your own data.

You can download the information you access on to your computer and then read it, store it or print it out as you wish.

EQUIPMENT

It is sensible to have a reasonably powerful PC for tele-working in order to use a modem, for example, a 386. You also need to buy the modem and communications software necessary to run it. If you have a fax you can use a modem to send faxes down a phone line, but you can also buy a computer fax 'card' which will slot inside your computer and enable your computer to send and receive faxes directly on to its screen.

If you are about to buy a modem or a fax card, make sure that you explain to the seller exactly what kind of machine you have. If you want to buy a fax card see if you can get an expert to fit it and set it up.

ADVANTAGES AND DISADVANTAGES

These apply to anyone who works from home but are particularly relevant for those people who are still employed by their main place of work.

The *advantages* are that within the dictates of the job you can set your own hours and work in your own surroundings. You do not have to travel to work each day and do not have a supervisor or boss hanging over you.

The *disadvantages* are loneliness and lack of discipline. People who are used to working with many other people often miss the day-to-day contact with others. They talk to their customers but rarely meet them even if they work closely together. Imogen Bertin says:

> As far as teleworking's concerned I've had customers I've never met. I have a customer at the Royal Society of Chemistry in London whom I have met once for 10 minutes and we've done 8 books together. I've designed and laid out the books, and done all the covers and so on, and we've sent to and fro all the 8 books including a 200-page book containing lots of really exciting chemical spectra.

Some people miss the stimulation and gossip of office life. Firms who do employ teleworkers are aware of this problem and try to arrange meetings or conferences for their teleworkers at regular intervals so that they feel in touch with other people. The Telecottage Association and its magazine *Teleworker* act as a link for teleworkers, and a forum for ideas and advice.

Discipline is something that you must get to grips with. You must be as reliable working from home as you would be in the office. Although your hours may be more flexible, you will still be expected to be on call within certain time limits.

If you have a job where you need to be in contact with the public by phone you will need to be available during certain times. That means you must organise your home life so that you are not disturbed during those times. If you can work flexible hours you must still be aware of when you can contact other people and not allow your home life to interfere with this.

It is difficult to work from home unless you can organise yourself, because you will always be torn between work and the demands of home life.

EARNINGS

Your earnings will depend entirely on what job you are doing. If you are still working for your employer then you will continue to get your salary as long as you do the same work and work the same hours. Self-employed people will be paid according to the nature of their job.

14

CATCHING YOUR CLIENTS

MAKING MONEY from your PC at home is all very well, but unless other people know you are there and what you can offer you are not likely to prosper. As any business person can tell you, you need good publicity just as much as you need a reliable product.

PROFESSIONAL ATTITUDE

You must take a professional attitude to marketing your business. You must set aside a regular amount of time for concentrating on the publicity and selling side of your business. Scrappy attempts to drum up new customers at infrequent intervals will not increase your business. It is no good telling yourself that you are primarily a subscription handler, creative writer, heraldic chart producer and that you haven't got time to spare to publicise your work. Without regular effort on marketing you will find that you won't be in business long.

MARKET RESEARCH

Your first task should be to find out who your potential customers are. Are you going to do something that people want? You can do this by asking friends and neighbours, conducting a survey by post or by posting leaflets through doors asking if anybody is interested in the service or product you hope to offer. You could also put a classified ad in your local paper to see what kind of response you get.

If you are aiming mainly at other businesses then approach them by letter or phone to find out whether they would be interested in purchasing your services or product. When you are sure that there is a market for your business then you must start organising publicity.

> ☐ **Take Michael Cattell's advice: 'Start small, don't be too ambitious.'**

Business paperware

Your professional attitude extends to what kinds of paperware you use to send out letters and publicity information. The minimum you will require is headed notepaper on good quality 80 gm or more weight paper, matching DL (business envelopes), business cards and compliment slips. Use white not manila envelopes for the professional look. Manila envelopes are for bills.

If you do not feel confident of choosing a design for your letterhead yourself ask your printer to help you. Printers often have a number of designs to choose from. If in doubt choose a plain heading. You should look businesslike rather than flashy. Local printers often sell complete business packs of 200 each of envelopes, headed notepaper, compliment slips and business cards in a choice of basic designs. This would make a reasonable starting point. Presenting yourself in a professional way on paper is all part of making sure that you and your business are remembered.

FACE-TO-FACE SELLING

Some of your potential customers may ask to meet you before they agree to use your services. Do not duck out of this kind of face-to-face meeting. Some people who may have thought twice about doing business with a newcomer may change their minds if you can present a professional and competent image to them.

Wear something appropriate. This does not mean that you have to turn up in a suit, but you should look smart and tidy. However wildly you might dress at home when in front of your PC (probably jeans and jumper like the rest of us!), your future customers will expect you to look respectable. It is simply common sense and courtesy. A neat appearance will make you seem reliable and help you feel confident.

Take samples of your work or a leaflet about your services to leave behind. Be prepared to answer reasonable questions about your work.

Women should take sensible precautions when visiting potential customers. Women, like Suzy Lamplugh, have disappeared while out meeting clients. If you cannot take a male friend with you, at least leave details of whom you are to meet, where and when with a friend or member of your family. Decide on a time for them to phone you at the meeting if you have not returned home.

USING THE PHONE

The telephone is not only ubiquitous but necessary to most business operations. But many people are scared of using the phone either to approach new customers or to talk to existing ones. Cold calling in particular terrifies many people. But you may well need to make such calls if you want new customers. If a new business opens in your town you will want to offer *your* direct mail services or whatever before anyone else. If you wait to write a letter you may be pipped at the post by a less nervous competitor.

Calm your nerves by following these simple rules:

- take some deep breaths beforehand;
- prepare what you want to say — write notes on a postcard, if necessary;
- practise your call into a tape recorder;
- make sure that you speak to the right person;
- introduce yourself in a few words;
- stick to no more than three main points
  1. what your business is
  2. what you can offer that other similar businesses can't
  3. the fact that you want their custom;
- be brief;
- speak clearly.

If you get 'no' for an answer don't take it personally. Just say 'Thank you for letting me talk to you' and go on to the next call.

COSTS AND MATERIALS

Working from home means that you cannot afford the large-scale advertising that major businesses use. But there are many ways to get publicity without spending a fortune. Your major costs will be computer paper (cut, not joined), photocopying and stamps. If your computer paper is of a good standard then you can use that for advertising leaflets and letters. If not then good photocopies will suffice. If you need a large number of leaflets then ask your local printer for a quote.

☐ **Many small printers now offer cut price packages of leaflets or letters for small businesses. In any case it will be cheaper in the end to use a printer for long runs of your leaflet or letter.**

Work out a list of potential clients and then estimate the number of leaflets or letters you might need. Always allow a few extra. Letters may need envelopes or you may want to use them like leaflets and post them through doors folded. If you are advertising locally contact your local paper and find out how much they would charge for including your leaflet in a copy of their paper.

USE YOUR COMPUTER

Your computer is the ideal tool for organising your own publicity material. Use the templates or style sheets if they are provided with your word processing package. Modify them to design a leaflet or letter of your own. Make sure that any material you send out has your name, address, phone and fax number on it. You should include your business name and address as publisher in small print at the bottom of leaflets or brochures. This is a legal requirement. In the same way, if you use a printer the printer's name and address, as well as that of the publisher, should appear on the leaflet to comply with the law. Post or deliver these to as many potential clients as possible (see also page 109).

ADVERTISING

Large-scale advertising may be beyond you, but a small classified ad in your local paper will not. Remember that as a business you will have to pay the trade rates.

Michael Cattell found that it is important to advertise in the right media for your work:

> Advertising is very important. You must advertise in
> the right place. I wanted to get into people's homes. I
> tried advertising in shop windows but that wasn't very
> successful. Then I advertised in the local classified ads
> paper which has worked very well. Try to find a paper
> that people sit down and read, and not just on the day
> it's published.

Any magazines that cater for your speciality can be approached for details of their small ad rates. While this will not get you nationwide coverage, it should bring in some interested enquiries.

If these enquirers do not use your services, you should still keep a note of their name, address and phone number to add to your mailing list, even if this is simply a list in a file rather than on a database. That way you can continue your publicity throughout the year. At regular intervals, say twice yearly or if you have something new to offer, send information to everyone on your mailing list. Don't forget to send information a month or two before Christmas if you can offer a special seasonal service.

LETTERS TO THE PRESS

There is nothing to stop you praising yourself – but subtly! At every opportunity write to the press about any subject related to your business. Keep the letters short and to the point, and always sign yourself with your business name, e.g. 'Sally Jones, Proprietor of Gnomewear'. The local press in particular like letters with a local interest, so try to angle each letter to the local press to a local person or place. When your letters are printed they will have your name and address underneath and, with luck, your business. You may get letters or enquiries this way to add to your mailing list. At the very least it keeps your name and business in the public eye.

NEWS RELEASES

News releases have been discussed in detail in Chapter 10. If you are good at your own publicity then it is certainly a marketable skill.

You should send out your own news releases whenever you have taken part in a noteworthy event. For example, 'Desktop publisher helps schoolchildren produce newspaper'; 'Lewisham poet wins national competition'; or 'freelance accountant's new overnight service' – or indeed anything of note in your business life.

You can see that most of the examples I have given are local ones. Certainly try the national press, radio and TV, but unless you are lucky they will not be interested. Your local press and radio are more likely to be, and there is the chance that the national press may pick up your story if they see it featured locally. (See page 156.)

LEAFLETS AND SALES LETTERS

Produce your own leaflets and sales letters featuring your services. Again this has been discussed more fully in Chapter 10. Use your computer to help you produce these.

DIRECT MAIL

You can send your leaflets out directly to people on your own mailing list. If you have a mail merge programme on your computer then personalising these letters will be easy. You can buy commercial mailing lists geared to your own interests but these can be expensive. Some lists come on a computer disk, while others can be sent on sticky labels ready for attaching to your envelopes. Some firms will even undertake to produce the letter and send it out to an agreed list, but this will probably be too expensive until you are well established.

BUSINESS CARDS

People often misunderstand the use of business cards and, if they have them, only hand them out on rare occasions to special people. They are not expensive to produce, so buy as many as you can afford. Keep the design simple whether you design it yourself or choose one of your printer's stock styles.

It should contain the usual name, address, phone and fax number, and your business name. If you want to add a description keep it short such as 'Qualified genealogist' or 'Database expert' if the nature of your business is not immediately obvious from the name.

When you have got your cards always carry some and hand them out to anyone who might be even vaguely interested in your work. A business person may file it and come back to you months later. Other people may pass them on or store them for later use or contact you for further information.

When you hand out cards you will often receive one back. Keep them and add the details to your mailing list.

☐ Avoid the business cards you can buy in small numbers by putting coins in a machine in shops. These cards are poorly designed and will be expensive if you try to get large numbers of them done in this way. They look cheap and will not impress clients.

POSTCARDS

Postcards are relatively cheap to produce if you only want a single colour. They are an effective and original way of advertising your business. Order as many as you can afford and send them to friends, relatives and potential customers. Pin them to noticeboards, leave them in hotels and waiting rooms, and post them through doors.

People like postcards and will save them or send them on, thus increasing the number of enquirers you hear from. On the front of the cards you could put your logo (design a simple one), and your business name and address. The back could have details of your business and a form to fill in with the enquirer's name and address on one half, and your name and address on the address section so that enquirers can send the card to you. If you are feeling generous you could stamp some cards.

Otherwise, on the correspondence half put your business information and leave the address space blank so that the recipient can send it on or you can send it to other people.

BADGES

I'm not joking when I suggest badges. Everyone loves badges, especially if they are free! Your business logo, together with the name and phone number, will be all you need. A badge 38 mm across in one colour on white will not be expensive. Hand them out freely to everyone. Don't forget the children. They may not need your business but they love badges and their parents will get the message.

RADIO AND TV

Your efforts on radio and TV will best be directed to local rather than national stations. Unless you can think of something extremely visually attractive connected with your business, the national TV stations are unlikely to be interested. Local radio, however, does offer opportunities.

Send out your news release to local radio stations, preferably directed to the producers of particular programmes. Listen to the radio and decide which programmes are most likely to receive you well. If a radio station contacts you, it may ask you to give an interview over the phone or to go into the studio and do one live.

> ☐ **Have a list of about three main points that you want to make about your business and try to work them into the conversation.**

Take a deep breath and listen carefully to what the interviewer says. Try not to say 'er' or 'um' too often but don't panic if you do. Any kind of radio interview reaches hundreds of potential clients so do take any opportunity to be interviewed if it is offered to you.

> ☐ **Radio phone-ins can provide useful publicity. If you can offer expert advice on a question raised by another caller then phone in and offer it. 'My name is Jenny Jones. I'm a qualified picture restorer and I can explain what you need to do about that kind of picture.'**

WORD-OF-MOUTH

Word-of-mouth publicity can be very powerful. Talk to anyone and everyone about your business. Ask them to mention your service to their friends. And when you do a job, put that extra bit of trouble into it so that you acquire a reputation for being reliable, pleasant and the best at what you do!

15

THE BUSINESS SIDE

IF YOU WANT TO SUCCEED in earning money from your computer at home then you must be businesslike in your approach to such things as paying tax and insurance, and keeping records. You also need to consider such things as insurance for your computer and software, and security for your home and goods.

If you are using your computer at home to work for one employer then you will continue to be paid by that employer who will also take care of your national insurance contributions. You will continue to be taxed by the PAYE (pay as you earn) system. For other home workers, whether they are full-time self-employed or earning a bit extra to their main job, honesty and accurate record keeping is important.

RECORD KEEPING

It is a sad fact that 80 per cent of business failures are caused by inadequate record keeping. Small home businesses are more prone to this than others.

It is no excuse to say that you are not earning enough. You will need to keep records, whatever the size of your business, and however small your earnings, because your tax inspector will need to see them. If you employ an accountant they too will need to see a complete record of your business transactions.

Do not try to wriggle out of keeping accurate records and declaring your income. Tax evasion, not paying the tax you owe, is illegal. Tax avoidance, making sure you claim all allowances you are entitled to, on the other hand, is legal. But in order to make sure that the tax inspector believes your claims you must be able to show evidence of all your business income and expenditure.

What paperwork is necessary?

You need to keep all your receipts, copies of invoices, statements, cheque stubs, delivery notes and all other paperwork connected with your business. You might not always be able to get receipts for fares and postage so keep details in a small notebook to show the tax inspector. This will probably be accepted if the amount seems to be reasonable.

Invoices are bills and should be sent out for each piece of work you do on your headed notepaper with a number or at least the order date. Send them out as soon as possible after supplying the work.

☐ **Keep a separate list of invoices and tick each one off when the payment arrives. That way you can keep track of how much money other people owe you and can send them a reminder statement to hurry payment up.**

Try to keep your paperwork in date order to make it easier for the tax inspector or your accountant to check it.

It is not difficult to keep simple accounts. Buy a cash book.

On a double spread use the left-hand page for income and the right-hand page for expenditure. Divide each side into columns like this for the left-hand page:

INCOME

date	invoice number	date paid	details	amount	VAT (if needed)

For the right-hand page your columns should be like this:

EXPENDITURE

date	invoice number	cheque or credit card number	details	amount	VAT (if needed)

When you provide your goods or services then you send out an invoice and record it in your cash book on the left-hand side. When you receive the money check it off. Do the same for invoices you pay in the right-hand columns. Record all ingoing and outgoing money.

You should keep a separate note of capital expenditure on equipment such as a new printer, which you need for your work at home. You may also need a separate business bank account.

If you are earning more than a few thousand pounds per year (and certainly if you are earning enough to pay VAT), then you are strongly advised to employ an accountant. It will be well worth the fee for the savings they will make you by being aware of all the allowances you can claim and by presenting your finances in correct order.

PAYING TAX

If you are still employed by one employer then you will continue to be taxed at source. If you are also earning some money from self-employment then you will be taxed on this separately under Schedule D, the same schedule as for full-time, self-employed people.

You must write to your inspector of taxes to find out if you will be considered as self-employed and under which part of Schedule D you will be taxed. Be prepared to show your financial records.

It is possible to present your accounts yourself. If you are earning less than £15,000 (1994 figures), then you will be allowed to send in a simplified account showing your profit in the form of total income less total expenses and allowances. For example:

Income	£13,500
Expenditure	£5,316.36
Profit	£8,183.64

If your income is over that amount you will need to send in complete details of your business finances.

☐ **If you earn less than a certain amount you are exempt from tax. This changes from year to year so check with your tax office.**

As a self-employed person you can claim allowances for certain things needed for your work. Claim all the allowances you are entitled to. These include such things as the cost of equipment necessary for your work, travel expenses, part of heat and light bills for a room used partly for your work, telephone bills for your work, subscriptions to professional journals, postage, reference books and so on.

If you use one room for working it is wiser to make sure that it is not solely used as an office or you may be liable for capital gains tax when you sell the property, as well as business rates. Agree with the tax inspector what proportion of your light, heat etc. you can claim.

It is also possible for someone who is fully self-employed to set off the loss from work in the accounting year against other income in the tax year in which the loss occurred and this can be carried forward. What this means is that it may be possible if you are making a loss from one business after deducting expenses to persuade your tax inspector to reduce your tax either on revenue in the same year or your tax bill in a future year. Obviously this is extremely useful and so the Inland Revenue have tight rules about where this is possible. This is where an accountant's advice would be useful.

If you are employed full-time during the day and your computer work at home is supplementing this, then you will still be taxed under Schedule D, but you will not be able to offset the expenses of your part-time work against your main work.

Capital costs

You can claim a percentage of capital items against tax. So if you buy a new printer for your computer for work purposes you can claim, at present rates, 25 per cent of its cost against income for the first year. This is called a writing down cost. Then you can claim 25 per cent of the remaining 75 per cent against income the second year and so on. So if your printer cost £800 your writing down allowance would be 25 per cent of that or £200 which you could set against tax. You would carry over the remaining £600 to the next year and could then claim 25 per cent of that as a writing down allowance. Any gain you get from selling capital equipment is subtracted from the carried over amount and any cost of extra equipment is added to the total. You can then claim a writing down allowance of the 25 per cent of that total. Ask your tax inspector for full details.

VAT (VALUE ADDED TAX)

If you start earning substantial sums you will eventually find you must register for VAT. This is an extra tax levied on goods and services. This means you must ask all your clients to pay VAT on your services, but you can claim back any VAT you have paid. Your tax office will inform you of the latest level of VAT. You will need to keep detailed records of your VAT separately and be prepared to show them to Customs and Excise (who collect it) on demand. It is at this point that if you do not have an accountant you may well find it helpful to employ one. VAT can be very complicated and time-consuming to deal with.

NATIONAL INSURANCE

If you are self-employed, you will have to pay national insurance under Class 2. This is a weekly flat fee. You can pay this to the DSS by direct debit, either monthly or quarterly. If your earnings are very low, you may be able to claim exemption.

If you are earning very little you may be able to claim exemption from insurance payments. Ask your local DSS office for a small earnings claim form. If you are exempt you will get a small earnings exemption certificate. Check with them for the latest exemption rate.

Once your earnings reach a certain level you will also need to pay Class 4 contributions. Fortunately there is an upper limit on these contributions. Your Class 4 contributions will be collected by the Inland Revenue and assessed at the same time as your income tax. Again you need to check how much you can earn before Class 4 contributions become payable. It is possible to get relief on Class 4 contributions if your business is running at a loss so check with the Inland Revenue if this is the case. You do not pay them after retirement age and your state pension is now unaffected whatever you earn.

☐ **The DSS issues a number of useful free leaflets giving advice to the self-employed. Read them and check the up-to-date limits for exemption purposes. The Inland Revenue also produces a leaflet called** *Tax-employed or Self-employed.* **Read this to find out whether you qualify as self-employed for tax purposes.**

Your tax is paid on the previous year so make allowances for this.

Business Insurance

Your home contents insurance will not usually cover your computer equipment for work purposes. Fortunately there are one or two specialist insurers who cater for self-employed homeworkers, such as Tolsen Messenger and London and Edinburgh Insurance Group (see 'Useful addresses', below). Their rates are within the scope of small home businesses.

The London and Edinburgh policy is called Homework, and is a combined policy which includes home contents and personal possessions as well as small business cover. Tolsen Messenger's policy is specifically for home-based businesses and is separate from your house contents cover. Both policies offer the usual small business cover including loss or damage to equipment in or away from home, loss of data and business money, liabilities and business interruption. One company, Daved Sanders Associates, provides a policy called Teleworkers Insurance which provides cover for teleworkers' business and equipment at several different levels.

There are some insurance policies that the law requires you to have. There are two that are most likely to be relevant to your home computer work. One is employers' liability insurance which you will need if you employ anyone on your premises. For example, you might employ someone to key in data on one computer while you extract information from another one. You must also have adequate insurance for any vehicles used in business. So if you use your car for carrying business goods and equipment make sure you have the correct policy. If you are seeing clients on the premises you will need to make sure that they are covered by your home accident insurance. If not, you will need to take out a separate policy. Check with your council to see whether you need planning permission to run your business from home. This is unlikely, unless you are causing distress to the neighbours or your work involves alterations to your home.

SECURITY

Most computer insurance policies will demand that your house has locks on doors and windows that conform to a particular standard. You must make sure that you follow the advice of the insurance company and get the appropriate locks fitted otherwise you may not get insurance or it may become invalid.

☐ **If possible, locate your PC in an upstairs room which doesn't face the street. If this is not possible then keep curtains or a blind drawn in such a way as to hide your machine from opportunist burglars.**

You can take steps to secure your computer either by an internal or external alarm or by physically fastening it to the desk with a specially designed mechanical device. You can find these for sale in large PC stores or catalogues. Consider having your PC and printer etched with your postcode. It is also possible to get your PC's circuit board etched.

OTHER CONCERNS

You may need to be aware of the Trade Descriptions Act 1968, the Sale of Goods Act 1979 and the Data Protection Act

1984 (discussed in more detail in Chapter 5). Basically you must be honest about how you describe your goods or service, and they must be of saleable quality and fit for the purpose (no disks with bugs – faults – in them). Keep to your delivery or completion dates and register with the Office of Data Protection Register if you are keeping personal details on your PC. Ask at your local library for copies of these Acts or books describing them in lay person's language. In short, honesty and reliability are the key. If you are a member of a trade or professional organisation they will also have rules which you should abide by.

16

TRAINING

YOU ALREADY HAVE A PC sitting in your home, so you may have a number of keyboard and program user skills. But most people can benefit from some training. It is possible to teach yourself a great deal on your own, but it is time-consuming and not always satisfactory. The quickest way to learn is usually to have hands-on experience under the guidance of an expert and be able to ask questions.

Even if you feel competent in one area of computer skills you may decide to work in an area in which you are not familiar. For example, if you are good at using word processing programs but want to use databases or spreadsheets then you may need training in using the new programs.

Here are some of the ways you can get training.

SELF-HELP

It is possible to teach yourself computer skills by reading the manuals that come with the programs and trying out skills on the computer. If your computer was bought second hand and you have programs without the manual then you are going to find it difficult. But be wary of buying a PC second hand which has software already installed but where you are not given all the accompanying literature, including the software licences, and disks. Software is licensed for use by one person. You can use programs bought second hand only if the previous owner does not retain any copies. Having said that, many programs can be learnt intuitively nowadays, especially if they use the Windows environment, but when things confuse you or the program goes wrong there is nothing to refer to.

If you want to teach yourself, try to get hold of the manuals for your program and computer, and work through them.

When you are buying new programs check that the manual is included. Indeed, you may want to judge a program partly on how useful the manual is. No program is going to be much use to you if there is no way of understanding it.

Many software packages now include a teaching program for you to work through. This tutorial takes you through the basic skills needed to use the program and tells you how to get help. The effectiveness depends on your willingness to concentrate and on how well written the course is. One of the advantages of these programs is that you can repeat them as often as necessary.

There are now specially designed software packages for teaching aspects of PC use which you can buy separately from the main PC utilities.

If you want to offer specialist skills such as accountancy, simply learning to use a spreadsheet will not be enough. You will also need to obtain some training in accountancy skills.

DEDICATED TUTORIAL PROGRAMS

These are programs on disk which are specially designed for teaching you how to use the programs you already have or aspects of using your PC. They are sold separately from other programs, and come complete with their own manual and disks.

If you find that the tutorial written into any of your present programs is inadequate then you may find one of these dedicated programs useful. They can be bought by post from ads in PC magazines and stores or borrowed from some libraries.

VIDEOS

There are now computer teaching videos on the market that tell you how to use certain programs, operating systems or computers. If you have a video these can be a useful supplement to your manuals. However, unless your video recorder is in the same room as your computer, you may have to rely on your memory. Several firms offer teaching videos for PC users. One such firm that offers a wide range of videos is Structured Learning (see 'Useful addresses' at the back of this book). Your library may have copies of similar videos which you can borrow for a small fee.

COMPUTER MAGAZINES

There are now a great many magazines catering for all kinds of computers, PCs, Amigas, Macs etc., as well as general computer magazines. There are also magazines specialising in computer games and software. Reading these magazines can answer some of your questions and give you information about useful hardware and software.

The ads in these magazines are also very informative and give you ideas about how you could use your computer to make money, as well as keeping you up to date with the new machines and software on offer.

However, unless you take out a regular subscription, the advice will be spasmodic for your particular needs. There is a magazine devoted to small home business users called *Micro-Mouse*. This is available on subscription (see 'Useful addresses'). Another useful magazine especially aimed at people earning money using a computer as well as a phone at home is *Teleworker*.

One problem with reading a lot of computer magazines is that all the software and computers sound wonderful, and you may be tempted to replace your computer and programs more often than necessary! As I have said before, you do not necessarily need the latest version of a computer or program to be able to use your computer to make money.

BOOKS

The computer industry has spawned a wealth of books about computers and software, much of it written in America. You can buy books on virtually any aspect of computers aimed from everyone from the most dedicated computer expert to a complete beginner. There are many books which give you a complete course in learning about any aspect of computers or any program.

Most of the books are straightforward to follow and have exercises to do so that you can practise your skills. However, they also tend to be very expensive and very bulky.

There are books aimed at beginners which give you less information but are easier to absorb. Even if you understand something about computers it is often more helpful to start with one less cluttered starter books and then move on to one of the more comprehensive manuals.

You may find that, as with the manuals, you only need to study part of the book to get going. You can work quite happily until you need to know something specific and then you can look it up. This saves you from having to go through the whole manual before starting work.

HELP-LINE

When you buy a new software program you may be offered the use of a help-line either free or for a fee. This means you are given a phone number to call so that you can ask experts for advice if you have a problem using your software and they will give you an answer over the phone. Some companies give you a few months free and then charge for the service. Other companies give you the chance to use a help-line but charge from the start. Paying for any help-line service can become very expensive so you must decide whether you are likely to use it often enough to justify the cost.

A help-line is all right if the expert can solve your problem. They cannot always do this, especially as they cannot see the screen and have to rely on what you tell them. Also, if you pay for the line you may not use it and it is not cheap.

If you have friends with a similar computer and the same software you could ask them to show you how to use it. This has the advantage of allowing you to ask questions and to get some hands-on experience. Your friends will also have encountered problems which they can then explain to you and so help you avoid them.

☐ **Many small clubs and societies will be willing to teach you how to use their PC if you volunteer to help with their accounts, membership list or newsletter.**

COMPUTER CLUBS

There are now a great many computer clubs run by enthusiasts that cater for different types of computer, use or software. You can find their addresses in computer magazines or ask at your library.

The advantage of joining a club is that you have access to a group of people who can help you and who have probably encountered any problem you are likely to come across. Sometimes enthusiasts can solve a problem or think of an easier way of doing something when the experts have failed.

For people working on their own at home it can be a help to know that there is a supportive group of people out there who are using the same computer and software as yourself and can give you advice.

ADULT EDUCATION CLASSES

Adult education classes may be available in your area to help with such things as:

- keyboard skills, including touch-typing;
- word processing;
- spreadsheet use;
- desktop publishing;
- computer design;
- accounting skills;
- writing classes;
- using databases.

The advantage is that you get small groups of students with good access to the class computers, lots of hands-on experience and expert advice for a reasonable fee. Your commitment is to attend a term's or a year's worth of evening or day classes.

The disadvantage is that because many of these tend to be general courses, rather than on a specific type of computer or software, you may not get to use the software that you have on your computer.

This does not matter so much nowadays as software tends to be very similar in many ways and the general principles will apply to all programs. It can be a good way of finding out whether you can cope with or are interested in, say, DTP or spreadsheets and what various programs are like.

There are, of course, also classes in related skills such as writing or bookkeeping or graphic design which can help you improve your skills for when you work with a computer.

COMMERCIAL COURSES

Commercial organisations offer courses on particular aspects of computer use or particular software, typically one or two days full-time. They do cost several hundred pounds but may be a good investment if you want to learn a particular skill to a reasonable standard quickly. They are often advertised in the national papers in the small ads.

17

IT PAYS TO BE HEALTHY

JUST BECAUSE you work from home don't ignore your working environment and habits. If your health suffers you will not be able to sit at your PC making money.

It is easy to become lax about your health while working with your computer in a domestic environment. You may also underestimate the time you spend sitting in one place and one position without the office procedure of regular tea breaks and lunch hours. What can you do to keep healthy and comfortable while using your computer?

KEEPING COMFORTABLE

Anyone who sits at a computer for a long time (or indeed anyone who is desk bound) must make sure that they are seated comfortably and are in a position to do their work without undue strain. Unless you take care about your seating and desk, and where you place your computer, you may end up with aches and pains which will inhibit your work.

Backs

One of the most common complaints of anyone who sits at a desk all day is an aching back. This can be caused simply by sitting in one position for a long time or by incorrect height of the chair or desk. This can lead to a curved spine.

First of all check the chair you are using. It should support your lower back, and allow your thighs to be supported along their full length without cutting into them and so inhibiting your blood supply. Your lower legs should be roughly vertical and your feet supported flat.

Many ordinary chairs are perfectly adequate for this. But if you are not comfortable, or your back and legs are not supported properly, then consider buying an office chair.

> ☐ **Cheap office chairs have backs that crack and slip, and are not adequately stable. The new versions have five supports at the base instead of four.**

If your feet do not lie flat on the ground then you may need to buy a foot-rest. A suitable box will do if it is the correct height, but a pile of books will slip.

If you are serious about keeping your back in top condition you can buy special 'back' chairs that support you in a semi-kneeling position and throw your back into the correct angle.

Hands, wrists and arms

When you sit on the chair you should be able to hold your arms roughly horizontally in comfort. Your desk, too, should be at the correct height so that you do not have to raise or lower your arms too much use the keyboard. The most comfortable height for a keyboard is about 12 cm lower than when you are writing. You can buy special computer desks which have a pull-out shelf below the tabletop to take the keyboard. Don't have your arms too low as that can be just as tiring as trying to type with raised wrists. You can be ruthless and chop the legs off your table to make it the right height but make sure they are all the same length afterwards!

If you find that your wrists and arms do start to ache when you type for long periods then you should consider buying a padded wrist rest.

☐ **Your keyboard may also be a source of strain if its keys are too stiff. You can easily buy a replacement keyboard that feels more comfortable to your touch – test it in the shop.**

Legs and feet

Anyone who sits at a desk for long periods may get swelling in the lower legs and ankles. Older women, unfortunately, are more prone to this. Poor circulation is the cause, and so you should make a point of moving your legs and ankles at regular intervals. Move your ankles in a clockwise, then anti-clockwise direction several times, and get up and walk around for a few minutes.

Check that your chair supports your thighs along their full length without cutting into them.

Eyes

Staring at a computer screen for a long time can cause eye strain – but then so can reading. You may get headaches or blurred vision if you stare at the screen too long. Rest your eyes on something else occasionally. Get your eyes checked regularly.

☐ **Have your eyes tested regularly. Many people do not bother and you may well find that a pair of glasses not only improves your vision but also reduces eye strain.**

Your computer screen (visual display unit – VDU) should be at a height where your line of vision naturally falls on the top half of the screen. You may be able to tilt the monitor but it is quite likely still to be too low without craning your neck. Raise the VDU on a book – a telephone directory is about the right height – so that you can look at it comfortably. Buy a paper holder to hold your paper at a comfortable viewing position at the side of the screen so that you don't have to keep moving your head or looking down.

Adjust the contrast and brightness on your screen so that you can watch it without strain. If your screen flickers too much you may need to replace it, although a certain amount of flickering is usual. Light characters on a dark background are easier to view.

You can buy a screen filter which can reduce glare and improve contrast or special spectacles which work in a similar way. You can also buy mesh screen filters which reduce direct and reflective glare. They reduce the contrast somewhat but are better than solid filters if you work near windows or bright lights.

Radiation

Expert opinion is divided as to whether staring at a VDU, your computer screen, for hours at a time causes any risk to your health because of radiation from the screen. There seems, on the whole, little risk of radiation overdose because the amount given out by a VDU is minute.

The Health and Safety Executive (HSE) does not consider

that enough radiation is emitted from a screen that users need to take any special action. However, if you are concerned about this many companies do make low radiation monitors.

However there are risks from staring at a screen for long hours. The first is the result of the flickering and brightness of the VDU. This can cause headaches and sickness. A screen over the front of the VDU can cut out this glare and flickering. More modern computers have less flickery screens and so you should buy the most up-to-date VDU you can afford. Most of us are stuck with the computer we already have. So, if you are prone to headaches, buy a screen for your VDU and take breaks from looking at it.

RSI

RSI (repetitive strain injury) has for some years been a cause of concern for office workers doing repetitive tasks such as typing. Unfortunately in 1993 a judge ruled that it was not a genuine medical condition, which was a blow to workers who had been so disabled by it as to be no longer able to carry on their jobs. In spite of this announcement workers suffering from RSI are still getting large amounts of money as compensation for their disability when caused at work. However, if you are working for yourself you have no one to claim from anyway!

If you find that you are getting agonising pain in your arms, wrists or fingers which cannot be accounted for by your doctor in any other way then you must consider that RSI may be the cause. Unfortunately there is nothing that can be done except take pain killers and rest the afflicted part.

However, at this stage I assume you do not have RSI and are in reasonable health. You should therefore take avoiding action.

☐ Do *not* spend all day using your computer keyboard. It will be counter-productive if you become disabled. Take regular breaks and do other tasks connected with your work – writing some publicity, walking to the library to do some research, going to interview a prospective customer.

The editor of a trade magazine offers this insight. When he arrived at a new office he found many people complaining of RSI. But these were journalists who had never had any keyboard training, and so held their hands awkwardly and typed jerkily. None of the secretaries who spent all day typing ever complained of RSI – but they were the only people in the office who had had professional training in the use of a keyboard.

☐ Take adult education classes in typing and keyboard skills, especially if you are going to be using your computer to type in a lot of text. Knowing how and where to hold your wrists and fingers will not only improve your output but will make you less likely to succumb to RSI.

GENERAL HEALTH

Don't neglect your general well-being. If you are working part-time at your computer don't work for such long hours that you get too tired to do your main job. Not only will your work suffer, and exhaustion could be dangerous in some jobs, but your work at the computer will not be good if you overdo it. You will start to lose business if your PC output is not up to standard.

Work out how much time you can usefully spend at your computer, including breaks, and keep to it.

> ☐ **Make time to see your family too – relaxation is important and you need the support of your loved ones.**

When you are working with your computer full-time from home it is just as important to take regular breaks. Do *not* spend all day at your computer. Without the routine of an office you will need to create your own timetable. Although this will be flexible it should include adequate lunch and tea breaks as well as a chance to go for brief walks.

Do not underestimate the value of fresh air. Working in a stuffy room not only dulls your brain but can contribute to headaches, sore throats and tiredness. Open a window, or take a walk in the garden or down to the library. Turn down the heating too: you don't actually need to work in the equivalent of a sauna.

General minor illnesses are nothing compared to the long-term consequences of a sedentary job if you are not careful. What you may be able to get away with when you are young will be harmful later. Middle-aged people in particular risk increased development of osteoporosis and muscle weakness if they spend long periods sitting down and this could mean they are seven times more likely to suffer hip fractures in later life.

Environment

As you are working with your computer at home you will undoubtedly be happy with your general environment. But there are ways of improving your working conditions.

Check that the lighting is adequate. It should provide good illumination without producing reflection or glare on your screen. If you work near a window move your computer desk to where the light is even. Try not to let a shadow fall over your work.

If you are working somewhere where noise is distracting you may need to consider moving your work to another room – or even the shed at the bottom of the garden! Turning on your own stereo may not do the trick and be uncomfortably loud for you.

> ☐ **Why not wear a personal stereo while working? This cuts out a lot of noise but, if kept at a reasonable level, still enables you to hear the phone or doorbell.**

Try to work at a desk wide enough for your PC and papers, and with room for your phone to be at easy reach. If possible have your computer permanently set out. If you have to put it away every evening you will be less inclined to get it out the next day and your productivity will suffer.

STRESS

Working at home can be just as stressful, if not more so, than working in a busy office. You do not have the day-to-day support of colleagues, and you can be lonely and feel under constant pressure because you are the only person who can do the work.

Relaxation techniques can be beneficial for keeping yourself in line. There are lots of useful relaxation activities – yoga, reading a book, listening to calming music, taking time out for a sport, lying in a bath, lying on a bed relaxing all your muscles in turn, having a massage. Find whatever it is that makes you feel relaxed and ready to go, then make room for it for 20 minutes in your day. Counteract the stress of loneliness by setting aside a regular period to visit a fellow homeworker or friend and join the Telecottage Association to keep in touch with what your fellow teleworkers are up to.

PEOPLE PROBLEMS

People can be a strain for many reasons but for the home computer worker these are exacerbated by your continual presence. Your family can feel neglected if you are in the house but sitting at your computer rather than talking to them. Make sure that you agree set hours with your family when you can work undisturbed, except for emergencies, on condition that outside those hours you will concentrate on your family. Try to arrange business calls within those hours.

When you are working, don't let your family disrupt you unnecessarily. If you want to make money using your PC then you need to have a professional attitude to your work. You *can* be more flexible than office workers (if the sun shines and you're ahead with your work you can go for a walk in the park), but in general you have to be very disciplined.

You may not be able to avoid business entirely at other times but make sure your family feel involved. You could ask the children to take phone messages, talk to your partner about work you are doing (but not all the time!) and work with the cat on your knee. Some people employ their partners in their work so you may like to consider this if your partner is not working and feels left out.

Loneliness

One 'people' problem is the absence of people. You may be plagued by your family when they are at home, but you may equally feel lonely when you are working at home during the day and your family is at work/playgroup/school. Answering the door to the milkman is no substitute.

Do not get bamboozled into spending long hours on the phone or nipping round to a friend for coffee just for the sake of company. If you cannot work on your own then maybe homeworking is not for you. Alternatively you may want to join with a friend in running your business, or find a club or class for an hour each day where you can mix with like-minded people.

READY TO START!

Now that you have taken your PC out of the cupboard and dusted it down you can put it to work. Any one of the ideas in this book can start you earning money from your PC.

Don't rush straight in. Take time to decide what PC work appeals to you and whether you will need extra hardware, software or training. Work out the start-up costs and see if you can afford them.

Don't be afraid to spend time getting to know your PC and practising your new skills for friends or clubs first to ensure that when you start your business in earnest you present a professional product to your customers.

All the ideas in this book can be put into practice by anyone prepared to put some time and energy into them.

Don't be afraid of your PC! With application of your computer skills, and attention to marketing and publicity, you can now turn your PC into a money-making machine.

FURTHER READING

Adair, John, *Effective Time Management*, Pan, 1993

Barrow, C. and Golzen, G., *Taking up a Franchise: The Daily Telegraph Guide*, Kogan Page, 1992

Bartram, Peter, *How to Write a Press Release*, How To Books, 1993

Bird, Drayton, *Commonsense Direct Marketing* (3rd edn), Kogan Page, 1993

Bird, Polly, *Sell Yourself!*, Pitman, 1994

Bird, Polly, *Tame That Phone!*, Pitman, 1994

BRAD (British Rate and Data), Maclean Hunter Ltd, annually

Clayton, Joan, *Journalism for Beginners*, Piatkus, 1992

Clayton, Patricia, *Law for the Small Business: The Daily Telegraph Guide* (7th edn), Kogan Page, 1991

Cork, Alison, *Profit Through the Post*, Piatkus, 1994

Crofts, Andrew, *How to Make Money from Freelance Writing*, Piatkus, 1992

Foster, Timothy R. V., *101 Ways to Get Great Publicity*, Piatkus, 1993

Golzen, Godfrey, *Going Freelance*, Kogan Page, 1991

Golzen, Godfrey, *Working for Yourself: The Daily Telegraph Guide to Self-employment* (12th edn), Kogan Page, 1991

Gooch, Brian, *The Computer Guide for Small Businesses* (2nd edn), The Computer Guides Ltd, 1991

Gooch, Steve, *Writing a Play*, A & C Black, 1988

Hawkins, Barrie, *How to Run a Part-time Business*, Piatkus, 1994

Huntley, Doreen, *Running Your Own Word Processing Service*, Kogan Page, 1991

Jackson, Tom, *The Perfect CV*, Piatkus, 1991

Jones, Graham, *How to Start a Business from Home* (2nd edn), How To Books, 1991

Lewis, Mel, *How to Write Articles for Profit and PR*, Kogan Page, 1989

Marshall, Peter, *How to Master Book-keeping*, How To Books, 1992

Mendelshohn, Martin, *A Guide to Franchising*, Cassell, hardback 1992, paperback 1993

Mills, Geoffrey, Standingford, Oliver and Appleby, Robert C., *Modern Office Management*, Pitman, 1991

Morris, Michael J., *Starting a Successful Small Business*, Kogan Page, 1993

Palmer, Robert, *1000 Markets for Freelance Writers*, Piatkus, 1993

Penfold, R. A. and J.W., *An Introduction to Desktop Publishing*, Bernard Babani (Publishing) Ltd, 1991

Penn, Bill, *Be Your Own PR Expert*, Piatkus, 1993

Phillipson, Ian, *How to Work from Home*, How To Books, 1992

Quilliam, Susan and Grove-Stephenson, Ian, *Into Print*, BBC Books, 1990

Taylor, Peter, *How to Keep Business Accounts* (2nd edn), How To Books, 1990

Treacy, Declan, *Successful Time Management in a Week*, Hodder & Stoughton, 1993

Turner, Barry (ed.), *The Writer's Handbook*, Pan Macmillan, annually

Wells, Gordon, *Making Money at Home*, Foulsham, 1991

Willings Press Guide, Reed Information Services, annually

Writers' and Artists' Yearbook, A & C Black, annually

Merlin Publications produces guides to different home computer jobs as part of its Success Library series. Contact them for information at Unit 14, Hove Business Centre, Fonthill Road, Hove, East Sussex, BN3 6HA.

The DSS produces a number of useful leaflets for self-employed people which give advice and information about national insurance contributions. Contact your local DSS office. The Inland Revenue produces a leaflet called 'Tax-employed or Self-employed?'.

There are a great many PC magazines on general sale. Check what your local newsagent has to offer.

BRAD and *Willings* are expensive so ask to see the latest edition at your local library.

The BBC's free leaflet 'Writing Plays for Radio' can be obtained from the Literary Manager (Radio Drama), BBC, Broadcasting House, Portland Place, London W1A 1AA.

USEFUL ADDRESSES

Abel-LABELS, Steepleprint Ltd, Dept B, Earls Barton,
  Northamptonshire NN6 0LS
The Arvon Foundation, Lumb Bank, Hebden Bridge, West
  Yorkshire HX7 6DF and Totleigh Barton, Sheepwash,
  Beaworthy, Devon EX21 5NS
Book-Builder, SPS Book-Builder Systems, Langton Villa, Langton
  Green, Tunbridge Wells TN3 0BB (tel: 0892 511110
  fax: 0892 514070)
British Franchise Association Ltd, Thames View, Newtown Road,
  Henley on Thames, Oxfordshire RG9 1HG (tel: 0491 578050)
BT Gold (tel: 0800 200700)
CFD: The Computer Freelance Directory, Freelance Professional
  Publications Ltd, 13 Priory Road, Newbury, Berkshire
  RG14 7QS (tel/fax: 0635 34869)
CIX (Compulink Information Exchange) (tel: 081-390 8446)
Desktop Publishing Today, Industrial Media Ltd, Blair House,
  184–6 High Street, Tonbridge, Kent TN9 1BQ
  (tel: 0732 359990)
Direct Selling Association, 44 Russell Square, London
  WC1 4JP
Enterprise, Entrepreneur Magazines Ltd, Haland House, 66 York
  Road, Weybridge, Surrey KT13 9DY (tel: 0932 829920
  fax: 0932 855741)
Federation of Small Businesses, 140 Lower Marsh, London SE1
  7AE (tel: 071-928 9272)
Freelance Market News, Cumberland House, Lissadel Street,
  Salford M6 6GG (tel: 061-745 8850)

Freelance Writing and Photography, Tregeraint House, Zennor, St Ives, Cornwall TR26 3DB

Graham & Son (Printers) Ltd, 51 Gortin Road, Omagh, Co. Tyrone BT79 7HZ (postcards)

Health and Safety Executive, Baynards House, 1 Chepstow Place,Westbourne Grove, London W2 4TF (tel: 071-243 6000)

Home Business, Merlin Publications Ltd, 14 Hove Business Centre, Fonthill Road, Hove BN3 6HA (tel: 0273 888992 fax: 0273 888994)

Home Run, Active Information, 79 Black Lion Lane, London W6 9BG (tel: 081-741 2440 fax: 081-846 9244)

The Institute of Direct Marketing (tel: 081-977 5705 fax: 081-943 2535)

Institute of Management, Small Firms Information Service, Management House, Cottingham Road, Corby, Northamptonshire NN17 1TT (tel: 0536 204222)

London and Edinburgh Insurance Group, The Warren, Worthing, West Sussex BN14 9QD (tel: 0903 820820 fax: 0903 20849)

The London School of Journalism (school), 22 Upbrook Mews, Bayswater, London W2 3HG (tel: 071-706 3536) and (admin) 1/4 Daniel Mews, Bathwick, Bath BA2 6NG (tel: 0225 444774)

Merlin Publications Ltd, Unit 14, Hove Business Centre, Fonthill Road, Hove, East Sussex BN3 6HA

Micro-Mouse, Broad Leys Publishing Company, Buriton House, Station Road, Newport, Saffron Walden, Essex CB11 3PL (tel: 0799 40922 fax: 0799 41367)

NUJ (National Union of Journalists), Acorn House, 314 Gray's Inn Road, London WC1X 8DP (tel: 071-278 7916 fax: 071-837 8143)

Office of the Data Protection Register, Wycliffe House, Water Lane, Wilmslow, Cheshire SK9 5AX (tel: 0625 535711 admin., 0625 535777 enquiries)

Office of Fair Trading, Field House, Breams Buildings, London EC4A 1PR

Personal Success, 239 High Street, Slough, Berks 1SL 1BN (tel: 0527 21878 fax: 0753 551305)

The Poetry Society, 22 Betterton Street, London WC2H 9BU (tel: 071-240 4810)

Publishing Magazine, 3 Percy Street, London W1P 9FA

Quartos Magazine, BCM Writer, 27 Old Gloucester Street, London WC1N 3XX

Small Business Bureau, 46 Westminster Palace Gardens, Artillery Row, London SW1P 1PR (tel: 071-976 7262)

Society of Authors, 84 Drayton Gardens, London SW10 9SB (tel: 071-240 4810)

Society of Indexers, 38 Rochester Road, London NW1 9JJ (tel: 071-916 7809)

Software Magazine, Edinburgh House, 82–90 London Road, St Albans, Herts AL1 1TR (tel: 0727 844555 fax: 0727 844202)

Structured Learning, 1 Twyford Place, Lincoln's Inn, Lincoln Road, High Wycombe, Buckinghamshire HP12 3RE (tel: 0494 452245 fax: 0494 450945)

Telecottage Association Membership (and *Teleworker*), WREN Telecottage, Stoneleigh Park, Warwickshire CV8 2RR (tel: 0203 696986 fax: 0203 696538)

Teleworkers Insurance, Daved Sanders Associates, The Old Post House, Bewdley, Worcestershire DY12 2AE (tel: 0299 401345 fax: 0299 404491)

Tolsen Messenger Ltd, 148 King Street, London W6 0QU (tel: 081-741 8361 fax: 081-741 9395)

Ty Newydd, Taliesin, Ty Newydd, Llanystumdwy, Cricieth, Gwynedd LL52 0LW

Universal Button Co. Ltd, 10 Wilton Street, London E2 6JX (badges)

The Writers Guild of Great Britain, 430 Edgware Road, London W2 1EH (tel: 071-723 8074-5-6)

Writing Magazine, PO Box 4, Nairn IV12 4HU

Writers Forum, 321 Pleck Road, Walsall, West Midlands WS2 9HD

Writers News, PO Box 4, Nairn IV12 4HU

Contact your local Training Enterprise Council for help and advice.

Details of PC users' groups are often mentioned in the many PC magazines.

INDEX